80 CAKES

FROM
AROUND THE WORLD

For the late Professor John Huber and Ernst Bachmann. For being the most inspirational and influential people in my culinary life; thank you for giving me the skills that made me the pastry chef I am today.

80 CAKES

FROM
AROUND THE WORLD

CLAIRE CLARK

A.

First published in Great Britain
in 2014 by Absolute Press,
an imprint of
Bloomsbury Publishing Plc

Absolute Press
Scarborough House
29 James Street West
Bath BA1 2BT
Phone 44 (0) 1225 316013
Fax 44 (0) 1225 445836
E-mail office@absolutepress.co.uk
Website www.absolutepress.co.uk

Text copyright © Claire Clark, 2014
Photography copyright
© Jean Cazals, 2014

Publisher Jon Croft
Commissioning Editor Meg Avent
Art Director and Designer
Matt Inwood
Project Editor Alice Gibbs
Editor Jane Middleton
Photographer Jean Cazals
Props Stylist Jo Harris
Indexer Zoe Ross

A catalogue record of this book is
available from the British Library

ISBN: 9781472907424

Printed in China by C&C Offset
Printing Co., Ltd.

A note about the text
This book was set using Sabon,
Modern No. 20 and Century Gothic.
Sabon was designed by Jan
Tschichold in 1964. The roman
design is based on type by Claude
Garamond, whereas the italic design
is based on types by Robert Granjon.
Modern No. 20 was originally issued
by the Stephenson Blake Foundry in
1905. Edouard Benguiat recreated
and updated the font in the
mid-1900s. The Century Gothic
font takes its cue from the geometric
sans-serif styles around in the 1920s
and 1930s.

Bloomsbury Publishing Plc
50 Bedford Square,
London WC1B 3DP
www.bloomsbury.com

Bloomsbury is a trademark of
Bloomsbury Publishing Plc

INTRODUCTION

When I first came to consider how to compile and select a personal collection of 80 amazing cakes from all around the world, the task that was set out in front of me seemed almost impossible.

There were just so many delicious choices from so many baking traditions! How could I possibly narrow down a selection from all across the baking globe to just 80 cakes, when deep down inside me I knew that I could easily include three times the number. Well, the truth is I simply had to settle on those cakes that I truly loved and felt would convey the wonder of the vast variety of cakes to be found from across all the continents of the globe. Cakes that I could happily cook and eat time and time again. Cakes that gave a sense of wonder and travel and occasionally eccentricity. But always cakes that tasted exquisite and that would be received with hungry appreciation.

Some classics such as the French croquembouche seemed like they might be an insurmountable project for most so I combined it with the simplicity of the modern cupcake and the fun of constructing something that doesn't take all day. I love the whimsical and the unexpected and I haven't been able to resist giving a few of the cakes my own personal take and twists. They might not be completely true to the tradition with regard to technique or ingredients but they will, trust me, be every bit as delicious as the originals. Some might even think more so!

We now appear to live in a world where we are all meant to love to bake. And more and more of us do indeed absolutely love to bake. I have been a pastry chef for more than thirty years now and so I couldn't be happier with the ever-growing love and fascination with the wonderful world of cakes and baking in general. And it is a world – a very wide world indeed! The cakes of France and Europe differ so very greatly from those sweet delights coming from the ovens of, say, Asia or the Middle East; different flavours and techniques bringing differing results but with one single unifying truth – they are all absolutely delicious to eat. I love the fact that cakes can incorporate flavours and ingredients as wide-ranging and diverse as almonds, walnuts and pistachios contrasting with cakes emitting heavenly scents of cinnamon, ginger and nutmeg; cakes with luscious soft cheese, the finest honey, plumped juicy raisins, glutinous rice flour, sweet potatoes, pandan essence, the freshest of tree-picked fruits and let's not forget those which are doused in the finest brandies, rums and wines of a locale. This is a world of passionate and creative bakers each creating a cake with their country's most treasured produce, expertly crafted and sculpted. A global cake heaven. My heaven and I hope soon to be yours too!

1

Rainbow Cake
Fiji

Hinduism, the second biggest religion on the island of Fiji, refers to the rainbow as indradhanush, *meaning 'the bow of Indra, the god of lightning, thunder and rain'. Apparently, those who have surpassed earthly ties are in a position to achieve the highest meditative state and experience the 'rainbow body'. Maybe that is why they named the beautiful reef that lies between the Fijian islands of Taveuni and Vanua Levu the Rainbow Reef.*

This egg-free cake is no mean feat to make. It takes time and dedication to produce all seven layers but it's worth it, so why not pull out all the stops for a special celebration?

You will need seven different shades of food colouring to create the rainbow effect. I like the small pots of gel colours, as they are very strong and don't affect the consistency of the cake mix. They are available online or from cake decoration shops.

Makes a 13cm cake

For 2 sponge cakes (repeat 2½ times to make 7 layers)
280g self-raising flour
2 teaspoons baking powder
1 teaspoon bicarbonate of soda
¼ teaspoon salt
400ml condensed milk
250ml water
2 tablespoons white wine vinegar
2 teaspoons vanilla extract
60g unsalted butter, melted
food colouring – red, orange, yellow, green, blue, purple, violet

Ganache
400ml double cream
700ml dark chocolate (70 per cent cocoa solids), chopped

Heat the oven to 170°C/Gas Mark 3. Grease two 13cm cake tins and line the base of each one with a disc of baking parchment. Grease the paper and dust the tins with flour, tapping out the excess.

Sift the flour, baking powder, bicarbonate of soda and salt into a large bowl. Mix the condensed milk, water, vinegar and vanilla together. Whisk into the dry ingredients to make a smooth batter, being careful not to over mix. Add the melted butter and mix in.

Divide the mix between 2 bowls, using scales to make sure they are both the same. Add one of the food colourings to each bowl with a wooden toothpick until you gain the desired shade, mixing it in thoroughly. Pour into the prepared cake tins, level the surface and bake for 20–25 minutes, until the sponge springs back when pressed lightly with your finger. Leave to cool, then remove from the tins.

Repeat twice more, using another 4 colours. For the seventh layer, make a half recipe to yield one tin.

For the ganache, bring the cream to the boil and pour it over the chopped chocolate. Leave to stand for 1 minute, then whisk gently to make a smooth, shiny ganache. Cover with cling film and leave to firm for 1 hour in the fridge or leave overnight at room temperature.

Sandwich the cakes together with a thin layer of the ganache between each one. Place in the fridge for 2 hours, then spread the rest of the ganache over the top and sides of the cake, using a palette knife to make ridges and ruffles. Await the gasps of surprise when the cake is cut open to reveal the rainbow of colours.

2

King Cake
Portugal

Part of every Portuguese family's Christmas, the king cake, or bolo rei, is a majestic ring of sparkling jewels. It made its way from France to Portugal in the nineteenth century, and is named for the dia de reis, *or Day of Kings, when the three wise men visited the baby Jesus. The round shape resembles a crown, the dried fruits the jewels. I use mango, papaya and kiwi fruit to add colour, along with other more traditional dried fruits. If you are making it during the festive season don't forget to include a dried bean. Tradition has it that whoever gets the bean has to make next year's bolo rei.*

Serves 6–8

30g fresh yeast (or 15g dried yeast)
100ml warm water (at blood heat)
500g strong white flour
5g salt
70g caster sugar
grated zest of 1 lemon
3 medium eggs
150ml dessert wine
100g unsalted butter, melted
75g raisins
40g soft dried mango, chopped
30g glacé cherries, washed and cut in half
50g sultanas
50g semi-dried apricots, cut into small pieces
1 dried bean (optional)

To decorate

1 egg, beaten with 1 tablespoon of milk, to glaze
200–300g mixed dried fruits, such as mango, papaya, kiwi, glacé cherries, figs, pears, sliced
50g flaked or chopped almonds
50–75g apricot jam
a little icing sugar

Mix the yeast with the warm water until liquid. Place the flour, salt, sugar and lemon zest in a freestanding electric mixer fitted with a dough hook. Add the yeast mix with the eggs and dessert wine and combine on a low speed for 1–2 minutes to form a soft, elastic dough. Add the melted butter and mix on a low speed for 15 minutes, until the dough is soft, shiny and pulling away from the sides of the bowl to form a ball. Remove from the machine and add the dried fruits, kneading well by hand. Cover the dough and leave in a warm place until doubled in size.

Turn the dough out on to a lightly floured surface and knead for 2–3 minutes. If you are including the bean, wrap it in cling film and knead it into the dough. Shape the dough into a 20cm ball and flatten it slightly with a rolling pin. Place on a baking tray lined with baking parchment. Using a 5cm pastry cutter, cut out a piece from the centre to give you a ring (you can bake the offcut and enjoy it toasted with butter). Loosely cover with oiled cling film and leave in a warm place until doubled in size.

Heat the oven to 180°C/Gas Mark 4. Brush the ring gently with the beaten egg wash and decorate with the sliced dried fruits and the nuts. Bake for 20 minutes, then check that the fruits are not colouring too much. If they are, cover the entire cake with foil. Cook for a further 15–20 minutes, until the cake is golden and sounds hollow when tapped underneath. Remove from the oven and leave to cool.

Heat the apricot jam until runny, then strain through a sieve. Brush the cake with the warmed apricot jam and dust with a little icing sugar.

3

Frog Cakes
Australia

The original frog cake was created in Balfours Bakery, Adelaide, South Australia. It has now reached iconic status and is even used to promote the state. Normally they come in green, pink and brown and have the same facial expression but I couldn't resist using a little creative licence and giving them goofy expressions. I tested them out on my ten-year-old nephews, Sam and Alex, who loved the sweet jam filling and soft sponge. I had carried them lovingly to St Pancras in a Tupperware box to eat on the Eurostar to Paris but they were gone before we even pulled out of the station.

Makes 20

200g unsalted butter, softened
200g caster sugar
4 medium eggs
200g self-raising flour
1 teaspoon baking powder
1 tablespoon milk

Filling
150g unsalted butter, softened
210g icing sugar, sifted
1 teaspoon vanilla extract
150–160g strawberry jam

To decorate
a little icing sugar
500g green ready-to-roll icing
1 tube of royal icing
1 tube of black writing icing

Heat the oven to 170°C/Gas Mark 3. Grease a 20cm square baking tin and line the base with baking parchment. Put all the ingredients for the cake in a large bowl and beat with an electric mixer until you have a smooth, soft batter. Spoon into the prepared tin and level the top. Bake for 25–30 minutes, until the cake is golden brown and springs back when pressed gently with your finger. Leave to cool in the tin.

To make the filling, beat the butter with an electric mixer until smooth and creamy, then gradually mix in the sifted icing sugar. Beat on a medium speed for 5 minutes, until light and fluffy. Mix in the vanilla extract.

Cut the cake horizontally in half and sandwich together with the jam, then cut into 4cm squares. Put the buttercream in a piping bag fitted with a 1cm plain nozzle. Pipe a small bulb of buttercream about 2.5cm in diameter on top of each square of sponge. Place the cakes in the fridge for 30 minutes to firm up the buttercream. Coat the sides of each sponge with the remaining buttercream, spreading it on with a small palette knife.

On a surface lightly dusted with icing sugar, roll out the green icing to about 6mm thick and cut it into squares to cover the cakes. Lay a square over the top of each cake and tuck it in around the sides, trimming off any excess.

Roll small, bead-like pieces of the green icing for the base of the eyes. Attach them to the cakes with a little royal icing. Now pipe 2 dots of royal icing on top of the green eye bases. To finish the eyes, pipe on the pupils with the black writing icing. Press the edge of a small cutter into the cake under the eyes to make an indentation for the mouth. Have fun giving them expressive faces.

4

Black Forest Gâteau
Germany

A Black Forest gâteau, or *Schwarzwälder Kirschtorte*, is not a Black Forest gâteau if it does not contain the ingredient after which it was named. Schwarzwälder Kirsch, a white liqueur made from cherries, comes only from the Black Forest region of Germany.
The combination of chocolate, cherries and cream with the cherry liqueur is irresistible. Originally red sour cherries, also from the Black Forest area, would have been used.

I have used black cherries and griottines, but do experiment and find your favourite.

Chocolate cake
200g caster sugar
115g plain flour
60g cocoa powder
½ teaspoon baking powder
1 teaspoon bicarbonate of soda
90ml crème fraîche
2 medium eggs
1 tablespoon milk
125ml cold coffee
50ml vegetable oil

Cherry filling
1 orange
425g can of black cherries
50g caster sugar
½ cinnamon stick
1 tablespoon cornflour

Syrup
100g caster sugar
100ml water
4 tablespoons kirsch

Whipped cream
500ml whipping cream
1 teaspoon vanilla extract
25g icing sugar

To decorate
250g dark chocolate (70 per cent cocoa solids), tempered (see pages 184–185), or Candy Melts (see page 188), melted
a little icing sugar
12 griottine cherries

Heat the oven to 170°C/Gas Mark 3. Grease an 18cm square deep cake tin and line the base.

Sift all the dry ingredients into a large mixing bowl. Whisk the crème fraîche with the eggs, milk and cold coffee until well combined. Make a well in the centre of the dry ingredients and pour in the wet mixture. Whisk just until a smooth batter is formed. Add the vegetable oil and whisk again to combine. Pour the mixture into the prepared tin and bake for 25–35 minutes, until the cake springs back when gently pressed with your finger and a skewer inserted in the centre comes out clean. Leave in the tin for a few minutes, then turn out on to a wire rack to cool.

Meanwhile, make the cherry filling. Peel the zest from the orange with a vegetable peeler. Drain the juice from the cherries into a pan and add the sugar, the juice from the orange, the orange zest and the cinnamon stick. Bring to the boil and simmer for 2 minutes. Remove from the heat, leave to stand for 5 minutes, then take out the cinnamon stick and orange zest. Bring back to the boil. Mix the cornflour with a little cold water in a bowl. Pour the boiled juice on to the cornflour, whisk to combine, then return to the pan. Bring back to the boil and simmer for 3–4 minutes, whisking continuously. Add the drained cherries, turn the mixture into a clean bowl and leave to cool. Make sure the cherries are completely cold before assembling the cake.

For the syrup, put the sugar and water in a pan and bring to the boil.

Remove from the heat and stir in the kirsch, then leave to cool.

Whisk the cream, vanilla and icing sugar to firm peaks.

To assemble the cake, cut it horizontally into 3 layers, set the base on a cake card and, using a pastry brush, soak it with the kirsch syrup. Spread the base with a 0.5cm layer of whipped cream. Put some of the whipped cream in a piping bag fitted with a 2.5cm plain nozzle and pipe a border of it around the edge of the cake. Fill the centre with half of the thickened cherries. Place another layer of sponge on top and repeat the process. Top with the final layer of sponge and press down gently to level the cake if necessary. Mask the cake completely with the remaining cream. Place in the fridge to chill and firm.

Meanwhile, make the chocolate shavings and curls. Pour the tempered chocolate or melted Candy Melts on to a marble slab and quickly spread it with a palette knife to level it out as thinly as you can. As soon as the chocolate has set, take a large chopping knife and, holding it at a 45-degree angle, push at the chocolate in an upward motion to make chocolate curls. It really does not matter if they are all sorts of shapes and sizes. If the chocolate breaks, it is because it has become too cold. Just scrape if off the marble, re-melt and try again.

Use the smaller flakes of chocolate to decorate the sides of the cake and the outer edge of the top. Pile the curls into the centre, dust with icing sugar and finish with the griottine cherries.

5

Torte Gianduja
Italy

Gianduja, a luscious, velvety, thick confection of hazelnuts and chocolate, was invented in Turin and remains a speciality of the Piedmont area. Flourless chocolate cakes are popular in this part of Italy. It produces some of the best hazelnuts in the world, which can be ground and used to replace the flour in cakes, giving them a dense, moist texture. This cake is stunning to look at and makes the perfect celebration cake for lovers of chocolate and nuts. I like to bake it in a bundt tin but you can also use a conventional round or square cake tin.

Makes a 23cm cake

200g unsalted butter, diced
200g dark chocolate (70 per cent cocoa solids), chopped
6 large eggs, separated
200g caster sugar
200g ground almonds
100g ground hazelnuts
10g cocoa powder

Caramel hazelnuts
50g caster sugar
50g toasted hazelnuts, chopped

Ganache
150ml double cream
200g dark chocolate (70 per cent cocoa solids), chopped

Whipped cream
250ml double cream
1 teaspoon vanilla extract
10g icing sugar

To decorate
1 sheet of gold leaf (optional)

Heat the oven to 170°C/Gas Mark 3. Grease a 23cm bundt tin with a little butter or oil, then dust with a little flour, tipping out any excess.

Melt the butter and chocolate in a large bowl set over a pan of gently simmering water, making sure the water doesn't touch the base of the bowl. Remove from the heat. Whisk the egg yolks with half the sugar until pale and fluffy. In a separate bowl, using a clean whisk, whisk the egg whites with the remaining sugar until they form stiff peaks. Mix the ground almonds and hazelnuts together, rubbing gently to remove any lumps. Fold the melted chocolate and butter into the egg yolk mix, then, using a large metal spoon, fold in the whisked egg whites alternately with the ground nuts.

Transfer the mixture to the prepared tin and bake for 45–50 minutes, until a skewer comes out clean when inserted in the centre of the cake. Allow to cool in the tin for 10 minutes, then turn out on to a wire rack to cool completely.

Meanwhile, make the caramel hazelnuts. Lightly oil a baking tray. Heat a deep, heavy-based pan over a high heat and add a tablespoon of the sugar. Stir continuously until the sugar begins to dissolve. Turn the heat down to medium and add another tablespoon of sugar. Repeat until all the sugar has melted and turned a golden caramel colour. Remove from the heat immediately and mix in the chopped hazelnuts. Pour out on to the oiled tray and leave to cool. When cold, chop the mixture into pieces.

To make the ganache, bring the cream to the boil and pour it over the chopped chocolate in a bowl. Leave to stand for 1 minute, then whisk to make a smooth, shiny ganache. Drizzle it over the cake and leave to stand for 10 minutes before decorating with the cream.

Whisk the cream with the icing sugar and vanilla until it forms firm peaks. Spoon or pipe it into the centre of the cake, then sprinkle the caramelised hazelnuts on top. Decorate with the gold leaf, if using, applying fragments of it with the tip of a small knife.

6

Bebinca
India

Bebinca is made by stacking up coconut pancakes and is cooked under a grill. Traditionally it has 16 layers but you can make as many as you have patience for. It doesn't matter if they are thick or thin.

This recipe comes from my dear friend and fellow pastry chef, Sanjay Gour. It is really delicious and keeps for a few days. He told me that when he was a boy in India, his mother used to make it because it was easy to transport in the bottom layer of his tiffin (a traditional Indian stacking lunch box). Thanks to Sanjay, I have not only this amazing recipe but also my very own tiffin.

You will need 12 egg yolks to make this. If you are wondering what to do with the whites, try the Steamed Chocolate and Strawberry Zebra Cake on page 152. Egg whites will keep for a week in a sealed container in the fridge and it's a good reason to experiment with making a different type of cake.

Makes an 18cm cake

350ml coconut milk
225g caster sugar
12 egg yolks
125g plain flour
170g ghee or clarified butter
30g flaked almonds, toasted

Mix the coconut milk and sugar together, stirring till the sugar has completely dissolved. Using an electric mixer, whisk the egg yolks till thick and pale. Mix in the coconut milk, then mix in the flour a little at a time, making sure there are no lumps.

Heat your grill. You will need an 18cm round baking tin at least 8cm deep, with a solid base. Put a tablespoonful of the ghee in it and put the tin under the grill until it melts. Take it out from under the grill and pour enough of the batter into the tin to form a layer 5mm thick. Put it back under the grill and cook till the top is golden, checking it frequently. Remove the tin from under the grill and immediately add another tablespoon of ghee; it will melt. Now pour another 5mm-thick layer of batter into the pan and cook under the grill till golden. Repeat the layering process till all the batter is used up. The last layer must be ghee.

Turn the bebinca out on to a chopping board and decorate with the toasted flaked almonds.

Black Russian Cake
Russia

You can imagine my disappointment when I discovered that this cake appears to be an American invention. Even worse, most recipes call for a packet of yellow cake mix and a packet of chocolate pudding mix. Things get considerably better when you make it from scratch and douse it in vodka and coffee liqueur. My apologies to Russia for suggesting it is a Russian cake; however, it is drowned in fabulous vodka, so has a certain claim to the name. The results are lethal but oh so delicious.

Makes a 25cm cake

60g unsalted butter
200g plain flour
50g cornflour
25g milk powder
90g cocoa powder
1 teaspoon baking powder
1 teaspoon salt
450g caster sugar
210ml vegetable oil
170ml whole milk
4 large eggs
60ml vodka
30ml Kahlúa liqueur

Syrup
45g unsalted butter, diced
2 tablespoons water
90g caster sugar
100ml Kahlúa liqueur
100ml vodka

Cream filling
300ml double cream
25g icing sugar
95g chocolate hazelnut spread
   or praline paste

Heat the oven to 170°C/Gas Mark 3. Grease a 25cm bundt tin and dust with cocoa powder, tapping out any excess.

Melt the butter and allow it to cool slightly. Sift all the dry ingredients into a large mixing bowl and then sift again to make sure the baking powder is thoroughly combined with the flour. Add the oil, milk and melted butter and whisk until smooth. Beat the eggs with the Kahlúa and vodka and whisk them into the batter. Pour into the prepared bundt tin and bake for 45–50 minutes, until a skewer inserted in the centre comes out clean. Leave to cool in the tin for 25 minutes, then invert on to a wire rack and leave for 30 minutes. Meanwhile, wash and thoroughly dry the bundt tin; you will need it for soaking the cake.

To make the syrup, put the butter, water and sugar in a pan and bring to the boil, stirring to dissolve the sugar. Lower the heat and simmer until the mixture has reduced by a third. Remove from the heat and stir in the Kahlúa and vodka. Pour half the syrup into the bundt tin and then carefully return the cake to the tin. Leave for 5 minutes, then invert the cake on to a serving plate. Brush the remaining syrup over it.

Whisk the cream, icing sugar and chocolate hazelnut spread or praline paste together until they form medium peaks. Spoon or pipe the cream into the centre of the cake, or serve separately.

Bacon and Maple Doughnuts
USA

My time working at The French Laundry restaurant in California led to all sorts of flavour profiles that I might not have tried otherwise. One of my breakfast favourites was a combination imported to the States from Canada: maple syrup and bacon, so good with buttermilk pancakes on a Sunday morning. Here I have combined the two with another American favourite, the doughnut. It really is delicious. The combination of salty and sweet with the soft, puffy doughnut is almost irresistible, and worth the time the dough takes to prove.

Makes 15

20g fresh yeast or 10g dried yeast
70ml whole milk
5 medium eggs
500g strong white flour
10g salt
60g caster sugar
260g soft unsalted butter
1 litre vegetable oil, for frying

For the icing
260g icing sugar
90ml maple syrup
2 tablespoons milk
1 teaspoon vanilla extract

To finish
200g streaky bacon

Place the yeast in a small bowl. Warm the milk to blood heat (37°C), taking care not to over heat it. Pour the milk over the yeast and stir until dissolved. Mix in the eggs.

Sift the flour, salt and sugar into the bowl of a freestanding electric mixer fitted with a dough hook. Gradually add the wet ingredients, mixing on low speed. Turn up the mixer slightly to allow the ingredients to bind together. Mix on medium speed for 3–4 minutes, until they form a soft dough.

Add the soft, pliable butter to the mixture a little at a time, mixing on a low speed and making sure it is worked in after each addition. This should take 15–20 minutes. The dough should start to pull away from the sides of the bowl and make a slapping sound as it forms a soft, silky, shiny dough.

Place the dough in a large oiled bowl, cover the bowl tightly with cling film and place in the fridge for at least 4 hours. For best results and ease of handling, leave it to prove slowly overnight in the fridge.

The next day, roll the dough out on a floured work surface to 1.2cm thick. Cut out rounds with a 5cm cutter, then remove the centre of each one with a 1cm cutter to form a ring. Place the rings and middles on a baking tray lined with baking parchment, cover loosely with lightly oiled cling film and leave in a warm place until doubled in size.

Meanwhile, make the icing. Sift the icing sugar into a bowl and, using an electric mixer, slowly beat in the maple syrup, milk and vanilla until you have a smooth glaze. Keep covered in a small bowl. Grill the bacon until it is very crisp and brown, then set aside.

When the doughnuts have doubled in size, heat the oil to 180°C in a deep-fat fryer or a deep saucepan. Fry the doughnuts, 2 or 3 at a time, for 2–3 minutes, then turn over and cook the other side. As soon as they are golden, remove them from the oil with a slotted spoon and drain on kitchen paper. Once all the doughnuts have been fried, fry the middles in 2 batches.

Dip the warm doughnuts in the glaze one at a time, then lift them out with a slotted spoon and place on a cooling rack. Repeat until all the doughnuts and the middles have been glazed. Place half a rasher of bacon on top of each doughnut and then put the doughnut middle on top of that.

For best results eat the doughnuts on the same day, although a little warming in the microwave is enough to refresh them the next day, if necessary. Try them with a scoop of vanilla ice cream or, for complete overload, wash them down with a Coke ice-cream float.

9

Accra Banana and Peanut Cake
Ghana

This cake is simply scrumptious. Banana, caramel and peanuts just happen to be three of my favourite flavours. Peanuts are grown in Ghana, so it seems perfectly logical that this is their national cake. If you can't wait to let it cool (I never can), eat it warm with lots of whipped cream.

The caramel sauce is best made the day before and allowed to cool and thicken slightly.

Makes a 450g loaf

150g unsalted butter, at room temperature
170g caster sugar
2 medium eggs, lightly beaten
210g plain flour
2 teaspoons baking powder
a pinch of salt
4 large, ripe bananas, mashed
100g salted peanuts, roughly chopped

Salted caramel sauce
150g caster sugar
150ml double cream (at room temperature)
½ teaspoon sea salt

To decorate
30g dried banana slices

First, make the salted caramel sauce. Heat a deep, heavy-based pan over a high heat and add a tablespoon of the sugar. Stir continuously until the sugar begins to dissolve. Turn the heat down to medium and add another tablespoon of sugar. Repeat until all the sugar has melted and turned a golden caramel colour. Turn off the heat and carefully add the cream (it will cause the sugar to boil up and spit). Return to the heat and bring back to the boil so the sauce becomes liquid again. Add the salt, pour the sauce into a heatproof dish and leave to cool.

Heat the oven to 170°C/Gas Mark 3. Beat the butter and sugar together until light and fluffy. Add the eggs a little at a time, beating well after each addition. Sift the flour, baking powder and salt together and fold half into the batter with a large metal spoon. Fold in the mashed banana, followed by the remaining flour. Finally, fold in half the chopped peanuts.

Line a 17.5cm x 11cm wooden baking mould (or a small loaf tin) with baking parchment and lightly brush with vegetable oil. Transfer the cake mix to the tin and level with a spatula. Sprinkle over the remaining peanuts.

Place the salted caramel sauce in a disposable piping bag, snip the tip off the bag with scissors and then inject the cake along the top with the caramel: simply insert the tip of the bag about a third of the way into the cake mix and squeeze lightly whilst pulling the bag out of the cake, allowing some of the caramel to come out on the top of the cake. I find 4 times is enough.

Bake for 25–30 minutes, until the cake is golden brown and a skewer inserted in the centre comes out clean. Allow to cool in the tin before turning out on to a serving plate. Pipe any remaining sauce over the top of the cake, sprinkle with the dried banana pieces and serve with whipped vanilla-flavoured cream.

10 Baileys Chocolate Potato Cake
Ireland

Who would have considered using potatoes in a chocolate cake other than a country that produces some of the finest potatoes in the world? Choose a floury variety, such as King Edward or Rooster. I made my first chocolate potato cake over 15 years ago for my friend, Claire Koffman, who was then working for the potato marketing board. I am happy to say that I still make the cake to this day, though I often change the finish and filling. This version includes Baileys Irish Cream liqueur. It is decadent, super moist and, in a word, RICH.

Makes an 18cm cake

50g good-quality dark chocolate (70 per cent cocoa solids), finely chopped
115g unsalted butter
200g caster sugar
2 medium eggs
½ teaspoon vanilla extract
100g mashed potato
110g plain flour
½ teaspoon baking powder
¼ teaspoon bicarbonate of soda
¼ teaspoon salt
120ml buttermilk
25g dark chocolate chips

Chocolate ganache
150g dark chocolate (70 per cent cocoa solids), chopped
150ml double cream
25ml Baileys Irish Cream

Chocolate glaze
6 gelatine leaves
120g cocoa powder
150ml water
250ml double cream

400g caster sugar

Baileys cream
150ml double cream
30ml Baileys Irish Cream
a few drops of vanilla extract

To decorate
300g mixed fresh berries

Heat the oven to 170°C/Gas Mark 3. Grease an 18cm topsy-turvy cake tin (or you can use a 20cm round deep cake tin). Line the base with baking parchment and flour the sides.

Melt the chocolate in a microwave or in a bowl set over a pan of simmering water, making sure the water doesn't touch the base of the bowl. Using an electric mixer, beat the butter and sugar together until light and fluffy. Lightly beat the eggs together with the vanilla, then add them to the mixture a little at a time, beating well after each addition. Add the melted chocolate and mix lightly to combine. Add the mashed potato and mix gently. Sift together the flour, baking powder, bicarbonate of soda and salt. Using a large metal spoon, fold these ingredients into the mixture alternately with the buttermilk. Fold in the chocolate chips, then transfer the mixture to the prepared cake tin and level the top with a spatula. Bake for 25–30 minutes, until the top of the cake springs back when lightly pressed. Leave the cake to cool in the tin for 5 minutes before turning out on to a wire rack to cool completely.

While the cake is cooling, make the ganache and the chocolate glaze. For the ganache, put the chopped chocolate in a small bowl. Bring the cream to the boil and pour it over the chocolate. Leave for 1 minute, then whisk gently to make a smooth, shiny ganache. Gently mix in the Baileys. Set aside at room temperature.

To make the glaze, soak the gelatine in plenty of cold water for about 5 minutes, until limp and soft. Sift the cocoa powder into a bowl and whisk in the water to make a smooth, thick paste. Bring the cream and sugar to the boil in a pan, stirring to dissolve the sugar. Remove from the heat and whisk in the cocoa paste. Gently squeeze excess water out of the gelatine and add the gelatine to the pan. Whisk gently until it dissolves. Pass the mixture through a fine sieve into a bowl and cover the surface with cling film. Leave to cool.

Whisk all the ingredients for the Baileys cream together until they form medium peaks. Cut the cake horizontally in half and spread the Baileys cream evenly over the bottom layer. Place the top back on. The ganache should now be cold and thick enough to coat the cake. If it isn't, put it in the fridge until it is thick but still spreadable. Using a palette knife, coat the outside of the cake with the ganache, making the surface as smooth as possible. Place the cake in the fridge for an hour to firm up. This is important so the glaze does not melt the ganache.

The glaze should have cooled but still be liquid. If it has begun to solidify, warm it very gently over a pan of simmering water, taking care not to let it get too warm.

Place the cake on a wire rack set over a clean tray. Pour the glaze over the centre of the cake in one go, letting it flow over the sides. It is best to use more glaze than you need to get a smooth finish. Any excess will fall on to the tray and can be used on another occasion; it will keep in the freezer for 1 month.

Leave the cake on the wire rack for 10 minutes, then transfer to a plate and decorate with the berries.

11

Bara Brith
Wales

Surprisingly, this cake has travelled far beyond Wales. Some Welsh migrants settled in Argentina around 1865, taking the recipe with them. A cake called torta negra, *or black cake, is popular in the Chubut Valley and is almost certainly an adaptation of the bara brith.*

A good bara brith always calls for the fruit to be soaked overnight in strong tea. The cake improves with age, and is really good three or four days after baking. Or you can serve it warm from the oven, with lashings of salted butter and drizzled with more honey.

Makes a 900g loaf

200g raisins
100g sultanas
50g currants
100g glacé cherries
100g dried apricots, chopped
300ml hot strong black tea
450g self-raising flour
170g light soft brown sugar
1 teaspoon ground mixed spice
1 teaspoon ground ginger
2 tablespoons marmalade
1 medium egg
3 tablespoons honey

Place all the fruit in a large bowl and pour the hot tea over it. Cover and leave for 24 hours.

Heat the oven to 150°C/Gas Mark 2. Grease a 900g loaf tin and line the base and long sides with a sheet of baking parchment.

Sift the flour, sugar and spices into a large bowl, make a well in the centre and add the fruit and tea, marmalade and egg. Mix well to combine. The mixture will look quite dry and firm. Press into the loaf tin and bake for 1½ hours or until a skewer inserted in the centre comes out clean. After an hour, check that the loaf is not too dark; if necessary, cover the top loosely with foil to prevent it burning. Let the loaf cool in the tin for 10 minutes before turning it out on to a wire rack. Warm the honey in a small pan and brush it all over the loaf.

12 Beetroot Cake
Poland

I took a little bit of a liberty here, as I know beetroot cake is not especially Polish. However, beetroot is used a lot in Polish cooking and I wanted to include this gorgeous cake in the book. I love the colour, and have decorated it with some very English candied violets, which add a surprising finish. For the photo, I baked the cake in an antique cake tin that I bought for a few pounds on eBay. You could use a pudding sleeve, which will come in separate halves. This recipe will fill half a sleeve. Alternatively, an 18cm round cake tin works just as well.

100g dark chocolate (70 per cent cocoa solids), finely chopped
250g cooked beetroot, roughly chopped
3 medium eggs
200ml sunflower oil
50g cocoa powder
175g plain flour
1½ teaspoons baking powder
200g caster sugar

Vodka syrup
75g caster sugar
75ml water
50ml vodka

To decorate
150g white chocolate
1 teaspoon freeze-dried beetroot powder, or a few drops of red food colouring
a little vegetable oil (optional)
30g dark chocolate (70 per cent cocoa solids)
candied violets

Heat the oven to 170°C/Gas Mark 3. Grease and flour the cake tin (see introduction).

Melt the chocolate in a microwave or in a bowl set over a pan of lightly simmering water, making sure the water doesn't touch the base of the bowl. Keep warm. Blend the beetroot to a smooth purée in a food processor. With the machine running, add the eggs one at a time, then pour in the oil. Continue to blend for about 1 minute, until smooth. Sift the cocoa powder, flour, baking powder and sugar into a large mixing bowl. Stir the beetroot mixture into the dry ingredients and then mix in the chocolate. Spoon into the tin and bake for 20–25 minutes, until a skewer inserted in the centre comes out clean. Remove from the oven and set aside for 10 minutes, then turn out on to a rack and leave to cool.

To make the syrup, bring the sugar and water to the boil in a small pan, then remove from the heat and add the vodka. If you are using a tin with a solid base, put the cake in the cleaned tin, pour the syrup over and leave in the tin for 5 minutes, then turn it out again. Otherwise, soak the cake with the syrup using a pastry brush.

Melt the white chocolate in a bowl set over a pan of lightly simmering water, stirring continuously to prevent overheating. Stir in the beetroot powder or food colouring. If the chocolate seems too thick to flow and coat the cake, add a little vegetable oil to thin it down, being sure to mix it in well.

Place the cake on a wire rack set over a tray. Spoon the melted chocolate over the top to cover it completely. Allow the chocolate to firm a little before using a palette knife to remove the cake from the rack. Place it on a sheet of baking parchment.

Melt the dark chocolate in a microwave or in a bowl set over a pan of gently simmering water. Use it to fill a small piping bag and snip a tiny hole in the end. Zigzag the chocolate over the cake to form thin lines. Sprinkle with the candied violets.

13 Belgian Chocolate Cake
Belgium

Belgium produces a colossal 172,000 tons of chocolate every year, of which 70,000 tons stay in the country. That's a whole lot of chocolates, pralines and chocolate cake. There is no definition of a Belgian chocolate cake other than that it must contain chocolate from Belgium. The ruffles and panels on this cake are optional – it will taste just as good without them but if you feel like a challenge, I promise you it will be lots of fun. The brightly coloured acetate transfer sheets for the panels are available online (see page 188) and won't break the bank.

If you don't want to temper the chocolate, use Candy Melts (see page 188) instead. Don't forget to check out your local supermarket or cake decorating shop, as many stock ready-made chocolate decorations.

Makes a 23cm cake

200g plain flour
200g caster sugar
¼ teaspoon salt
1½ teaspoons bicarbonate of soda
75g cocoa powder
150ml boiling water
320ml buttermilk
2 teaspoons vanilla extract
190g unsalted butter
350g dark soft brown sugar
4 large eggs, lightly beaten

Chocolate glaze
75ml double cream
20g caster sugar
2 tablespoons water
260g apricot jam, warmed and sieved
175g dark chocolate (70 per cent cocoa solids), finely chopped

Chocolate panels
1 patterned acetate transfer sheet
150g dark chocolate (70 per cent cocoa solids), tempered (see pages 184–185), or dark cocoa Candy Melts (see page 188), melted

Chocolate shavings
350g milk chocolate, tempered (see pages 184–185), or Candy Melts (see page 188), melted

Heat the oven to 170°C/Gas Mark 3. Grease a 23cm round springform cake tin, dust it with cocoa powder and tap out any excess.

Sift the flour, caster sugar, salt and bicarbonate of soda into a large mixing bowl. In a separate bowl, whisk the cocoa powder and boiling water together until smooth. Add the buttermilk and vanilla.

Using an electric mixer, beat the butter and brown sugar together for 3–4 minutes, until light and fluffy. Gradually add the beaten eggs a little at a time, creaming well after each addition. Reduce the speed and mix in half the dry ingredients, then add the cocoa and buttermilk mixture and blend without over mixing. Add the remaining dry ingredients and mix until barely combined.

Transfer to the prepared tin and level the top. Bake for 45–50 minutes, until a skewer inserted in the centre comes out clean. Leave to cool in the tin for 15 minutes, then turn out on to a wire rack to cool completely.

Whilst the cake is baking, make the chocolate glaze. Put the cream, sugar, water and jam into a pan and bring to the boil over a medium heat, stirring occasionally so it does not stick. Place the chopped chocolate in a bowl. Pour the boiled cream mixture over the chocolate, making sure the chocolate is completely covered. Let it stand for 1 minute, then whisk very gently to form a smooth, shiny glaze. Cover the surface with cling film to prevent it drying out. Allow to cool to blood heat.

Put the cake on a 23cm cake card and rest it on a wire rack placed over a clean tray to catch the excess glaze. Pour the glaze on to the centre of the cake and use a palette knife to push it over the sides. Make sure the sides are completely covered, spreading the glaze with the palette knife if necessary. Let the cake sit for 10–15 minutes so the glaze begins to set a little, then remove it from the wire rack.

Before you start to make the chocolate panels, have ready a palette knife, a small, sharp knife and a ruler. Place the transfer sheet on a piece of baking parchment that is 2.5cm bigger all round than the transfer. Pour the tempered chocolate or melted Candy Melts over the transfer and, with a palette knife, quickly spread it evenly over the transfer sheet. As soon as it is set, use the small knife and ruler to cut it into equal squares of about 5cm. Don't leave it too long or the chocolate will become too firm to cut.

To make the chocolate shavings, pour the tempered chocolate or melted Candy Melts on to a slab of marble and quickly spread it with a palette knife to level it out as thinly as you can. Allow the chocolate to

set and then, with a large chopping knife at a flat angle, shave it off the marble in roughly 5cm pieces. It really does not matter if they are all sorts of shapes and sizes. If the chocolate breaks, it is because it has become too cold. You can scrape it off, re-melt it and try again.

Lay the panels overlapping round the sides of the cake; they will stick to the glaze. To decorate the top of the cake, I always start about 1cm in from the edge and lay the pieces of shaved chocolate next to each other to make a full circle. Then I continue making slightly overlapping circles until I reach the centre. Depending on the shape of your chocolate shavings, you can make up your own design to suit.

14

Yemen Honey Cake
Yemen

Known for its medicinal qualities, Yemen honey is rare and expensive. The bees collect the nectar from the flowers of the sidi tree – the same tree that provided the thorns for Christ's 'crown of thorns'. I was lucky enough to try this liquid gold at a food festival in Dubai. Fragrant, golden and sweet, it was a truly heavenly experience. How I wish I had bought some at the time.

If Yemen honey is out of your price range, use any good-quality runny honey. This is not the easiest cake to make, but resting the dough thoroughly should help to make the layers as thin as possible.

Makes a 25cm cake

520g plain flour
7g easy-blend dried yeast
½ teaspoon salt
125ml lukewarm water
2 tablespoons milk
5 medium eggs, lightly beaten
300g unsalted butter, melted
340g honey
1 tablespoon black and white sesame
  seeds

Mix the flour, yeast and salt together in a large bowl and make a well in the centre. Pour in the water, along with the milk and eggs, and stir everything together to form a dough, adding 4 tablespoons of the melted butter. Turn the dough out on to a lightly floured work surface and knead until it is smooth, shiny and elastic. If it seems too wet, add a little more flour. You can make the dough in an electric mixer fitted with a dough hook if you prefer; it's less work but not as much fun. Cover and leave to rest in a warm place for 1 hour, until doubled in size.

Heat the oven to 180°C/Gas Mark 4. Grease a 25cm cake tin. Divide the dough into 7 balls, place on a floured surface, then cover with a damp tea towel and leave to rest for 30 minutes. It is very important to let the dough relax, as it makes it easier to work with. Roll one ball of dough into a 25cm circle. Place it in the greased cake tin and brush with melted butter. Repeat with the remaining rounds of dough, pressing the edges together to attach the rounds as you put them in the tin. Mix the remaining butter with the honey and brush a little over the top of the cake.

Bake for 25 minutes, until golden. Remove from the oven and pour half the butter and honey mixture over the cake in the tin. Sprinkle with the sesame seeds. Allow to rest for a few minutes, then serve warm, with the remaining honey and butter mix.

15 Black Gingerbread with Coconut Frosting
Jamaica

Jamaica is the third largest producer of ginger in the world. Its ginger is particularly fiery and is considered to have medicinal qualities as well as culinary ones. Jamaican ginger cake has long been popular in the UK but it's not clear whether it was invented by the Jamaicans or by the British, using Jamaican ginger.

I have used a moist, shaved coconut for the finish on this delicious cake. Wash it down with a large glass of Jamaican ginger beer.

Makes 12

225g unsalted butter
120ml water
180g black treacle
180g honey
155g dark soft brown sugar
385g wholemeal flour
1½ teaspoons bicarbonate of soda
½ teaspoon salt
3 teaspoons ground ginger
1 teaspoon ground mixed spice
2 teaspoons ground cinnamon
3 large eggs
120ml milk
15g fresh ginger, grated

Ginger syrup
100g caster sugar
100ml water
300ml ginger beer

Coconut frosting
250g cream cheese
60g unsalted butter, at room
   temperature
220g icing sugar
1 teaspoon vanilla extract
100ml coconut milk

To decorate
a little shaved coconut (or desiccated
   coconut)

Heat the oven to 180°C/Gas Mark 4. Grease and flour 12 individual pyramid cake moulds or a 25cm round cake tin.

Combine the butter, water, black treacle, honey and brown sugar in a pan and place over a low heat. Stir frequently until the butter has just melted and all the ingredients are well blended. Remove from the heat, pour into a large bowl and set aside to cool.

Sift the flour, bicarbonate of soda, salt and spices together. When the treacle mixture feels just warm to the touch, mix in the eggs, one at a time, followed by the milk. Fold the dry ingredients into the batter and then stir in the grated ginger.

Pour the batter into the prepared cake moulds or large tin and bake for about 18 minutes for the individual cakes, 45–55 minutes for a large cake. Check by pressing the top of the cake lightly with your finger; it should spring back. Allow the cakes to cool for 10 minutes, then turn them out on to a wire rack to cool completely.

Meanwhile, make the syrup. Put the sugar and water in a small pan and bring to the boil, stirring to dissolve the sugar. Remove from the heat and stir in the ginger beer.

To make the frosting, beat the cream cheese and butter together until fluffy, then gradually sift in the icing sugar, beating well after each addition. Beat in the vanilla extract and coconut milk.

Cut the pyramid cakes vertically in half and brush well with the syrup. Sandwich them together with a little of the coconut frosting. Using a palette knife, coat the cakes with the remaining frosting. Roll them in the shaved coconut.

If you have made a round cake, cut it horizontally into 3 layers. Place the bottom layer on a cake card and soak with the syrup. Pipe or spread a layer of frosting on top and level it with a spatula. Add another layer of sponge and repeat the process. Add the final layer of sponge and soak with the remaining syrup. Coat the outside of the cake with the remaining frosting, then decorate with the shaved coconut.

16 Barmbrack
Ireland

Barmbrack means 'speckled bread'. It is associated with a popular Halloween game where various small items, such as peas, little sticks, rings and coins, would be baked into the loaf. Each item had a meaning. You could be thankful if your slice contained a coin, as it would bring wealth, but a pea meant that you were doomed to remain unmarried or to be in continuous dispute.

Barmbrack is perfect for toasting over the fire on a cold winter afternoon. It will keep well in a tin for at least a week.

Makes a 450g loaf or 8 individual loaves

220g light soft brown sugar
200g sultanas
75g golden raisins
50g mixed candied peel, chopped
300ml hot black tea
160g self-raising flour
2 medium eggs
grated zest of 1 lemon

Put the sugar, sultanas, raisins and candied peel in a large bowl. Pour the hot tea over the mixture, cover and leave overnight, so the fruit absorbs the tea.

Heat the oven to 170°C/Gas Mark 3. Thoroughly grease a 450g loaf tin or 8 individual loaf tins. If using the large tin, line the base and long sides with a piece of baking parchment. Put the flour in a bowl, then add the fruit and any excess liquid. Add the eggs and lemon zest and mix until smooth. Transfer the mixture to the tin or individual tins and bake for 60–70 minutes for a large loaf, 30–35 minutes for small ones, until well risen and firm to the touch; check that a skewer inserted in the centre comes out clean. Leave to cool for 20 minutes, then turn out on to a wire rack to cool completely.

Serve sliced and buttered, or toast and serve warm with butter and jam – plum jam goes well.

17 Praline Croquembouche Cupcakes
France

The godfather of all chefs, Antonin Carême, is credited with inventing the croquembouche. A tower of caramel-crusted, feather-light choux buns crammed with vanilla custard, it's a magnificently engineered cake suitable for any celebration. Traditionally seen at weddings, it has also been modified and shaped into prams, cornucopias and a variety of equally impressive forms.

However, it takes a very dedicated baker to attempt a full-blown croquembouche, so I have come up with these adorable little cupcakes as an alternative. The little buns can be quite fiddly to fill, so you could just fill the cupcakes with the praline custard instead.

Makes 12

165g unsalted butter, softened
315g caster sugar
3 large eggs, lightly beaten
1 teaspoon vanilla extract
125g self-raising flour
90g plain flour
180ml milk

Praline custard filling
90g caster sugar
1 large egg
2 large egg yolks
1 teaspoon vanilla extract
15g plain flour
15g cornflour
250ml whole milk
2 tablespoons praline paste or chocolate hazelnut spread

Choux pastry
125ml water
125ml whole milk
100g unsalted butter, diced
½ teaspoon salt
½ teaspoon caster sugar
130g strong white flour
4 large eggs, lightly beaten

Caramel
300g caster sugar
1 teaspoon liquid glucose
3 tablespoons water

To decorate
sugarpaste flowers
hundreds and thousands

Heat the oven to 170°C/Gas Mark 3. Line a 12-hole muffin tin with cupcake wrappers.

Cream the butter and sugar together until pale and fluffy. Add the eggs and vanilla extract a little at a time, beating well after each addition. Sift the flours together and fold in with a large metal spoon, alternating with the milk. Spoon the batter into the cupcake wrappers, filling them just under half full. Bake for 20–25 minutes, until a skewer inserted in the centre comes out clean. Leave to cool on a wire rack.

For the praline custard filling, whisk the sugar, egg, egg yolks, vanilla, flour and cornflour together in a bowl to form a smooth paste. Bring the milk to the boil, pour it over the mixture and whisk until combined. Return to the pan and cook over a medium heat, whisking continuously, until the mixture thickens and begins to boil. Reduce the heat and cook for a minute more, still whisking. Remove from the heat and whisk in the praline paste or chocolate hazelnut spread. Transfer to a clean bowl, cover the surface with cling film and leave to cool.

For the choux pastry, line 2 baking trays with silicone mats. Heat the oven to 190°C/Gas Mark 5. Combine the water, milk, butter, salt and sugar in a saucepan and bring to the boil over a medium heat, stirring occasionally. Reduce the heat and add the flour, stirring until it forms a ball in the centre of the pan. Cook for 30 seconds. Transfer to a mixing bowl and beat with a wooden spoon for 1 minute to cool slightly; the mixture should be hand hot. Add the eggs a little at a time, beating well with a wooden spoon after each addition. Once all the egg has been added, the dough should be smooth, shiny, hold its shape, and drop easily from the spoon when gently shaken.

Spoon into a piping bag fitted with a 5mm plain nozzle. Pipe dots no more than 1.2cm in diameter on the lined baking trays, spacing them about 1.2cm apart. Dip your finger in water and press lightly on the buns to smooth any tips that might have formed. Bake for 15–18 minutes, until golden brown and crisp. Remove from the oven and leave to cool on a wire rack.

Fill a disposable piping bag with the praline filling and cut a small hole in the tip. Make a hole in the base of each choux bun with a skewer and pipe the filling into them. Lay them out on a clean baking tray.

Put all the ingredients for the caramel in a small, heavy-based pan, stir well and brush down the sides of the pan with a pastry brush dipped in cold water to remove any sugar crystals. Bring to the boil over a high heat without stirring. As soon as the sugar starts to turn golden, remove from the heat and dip the

bottom of the pan in iced water for 15–20 seconds to cool it quickly and prevent the caramel cooking further. Dip the top of each bun into the caramel and set them down on a baking tray lined with baking parchment. When the caramel on top of the buns has set, carefully dip the base of each bun in a little caramel and stack them up on the cupcakes. I start with a layer that covers the top of each cupcake, then build the next layer and so on. Stick the flowers on with a little of the caramel and scatter the sprinkles over.

18 Dobos Torte
Hungary

I learned to make this cake at college, while studying for my advanced pastry exam. It was invented by Jozsef Dobos, a leading confectioner, in Budapest in 1885. Apparently there are over a hundred variations, perhaps because Jozsef would not share his recipe until 1906, when he retired and donated a copy to the Budapest Confectioners Guild. I am sharing my college recipe with you. I cannot confirm whether it is the original or not but it is absolutely lovely and remains in my repertoire to this day.

6 large eggs, separated
150g icing sugar, sifted
1 teaspoon vanilla extract
130g plain flour, sifted
grated zest of 1 orange

Chocolate buttercream
120g dark chocolate (70 per cent cocoa solids), finely chopped
5 egg yolks
150g caster sugar
3 tablespoons water
225g unsalted butter, cut into 2.5cm cubes
a few drops of orange oil
a pinch of salt

To decorate
15 hazelnuts, toasted and chopped
150g caster sugar
3 tablespoons water

Heat the oven to 180°C/Gas Mark 4. Grease a 40cm x 28cm baking tray and line it with baking parchment.

Using an electric mixer, whisk the egg yolks with half the icing sugar and the vanilla until thick and pale. In a separate bowl, whisk the egg whites with the remaining icing sugar until they form stiff peaks. Using a large metal spoon, gently fold a third of the meringue into the egg yolk mixture. Now fold in a third of the flour. Repeat the process until all the egg whites and flour have been incorporated, taking care not to over mix and lose volume. Gently fold in the orange zest.

Transfer the batter to the baking tray and level the surface with a palette knife. Bake for 5–7 minutes; the cake should have barely any colour and should feel dry to the touch but not firm and crisp. It is so thin that it will keep cooking in the residual heat of the baking tray, so you have to act quickly and transfer it to a cool baking tray or a cooling rack. Run a knife around the edges to loosen it first.

To make the buttercream, melt the chocolate in a microwave or in a bowl set over a pan of lightly simmering water, making sure the water doesn't touch the base of the bowl. Using a freestanding electric mixer, whisk the egg yolks on low speed. Put the sugar and water into a heavy-based pan and mix well to dissolve the sugar. Wash down the sides of the pan with a pastry brush dipped in cold water to remove any sugar crystals. Bring to the boil over a high heat and cook without

stirring until it reaches 118°C (soft-ball stage) on a sugar thermometer. Pour it on to the egg yolks in a slow trickle, mixing on a low speed. Increase the speed to medium and continue to whisk until the mixture is pale and fluffy and barely warm. Add the butter a little at a time, whisking well after each addition. Remove from the mixer and fold in the melted chocolate, orange oil and salt.

Cut the cake into 6 equal strips. Set the first piece on a cake card and spread with a layer of the buttercream. It should be the same thickness as the sponge sheet. Place another piece of sponge on top, spread with buttercream, and repeat until all the sponge has been used. Cover the top and sides of the cake with the remaining buttercream, giving them a thicker layer. Press the chopped toasted hazelnuts on to the sides of the cake to cover. Put the cake into the fridge to firm up while you prepare the decoration.

Line a baking sheet with a silicone mat. Put the sugar and water into a heavy-based pan and mix well. Wash down the sides of the pan with a pastry brush dipped in cold water to remove any sugar crystals. Bring to the boil over a high heat and cook, without stirring, until it turns into a golden caramel. Spoon immediately on to the baking mat in irregular shapes and leave to cool and harden. Remove the cake from the fridge and decorate with the caramel shapes.

19

Dundee Cake
Scotland

The most popular story surrounding this cake is that Mary, Queen of Scots did not like cherries and so a cherry-free cake with almonds was created especially for her. The name came from the Dundee-based Keiller's marmalade company, who were the first to produce the cake commercially, and recipes often include a spoonful or two of marmalade. I have a wonderful old Dundee cake tin I bought for just a penny. I confess I made this recipe just the right size to allow me to use my tin in the photo.

Makes a 20cm cake

175g raisins
175g currants
65g candied pineapple, chopped
grated zest of 1 orange
grated zest of 1 lemon
100ml Scottish whisky
175g unsalted butter, at room
   temperature
175g light soft brown sugar
4 large eggs, lightly beaten
2 tablespoons orange marmalade
175g plain flour
1 teaspoon baking powder
1 teaspoon ground mixed spice
65g ground almonds
150g whole blanched almonds

Place the dried fruits in a large mixing bowl with the orange and lemon zest and pour over the whisky. Cover and leave to soak for 24 hours.

Heat the oven to 150°C/Gas Mark 2. Grease and line a 20cm round deep cake tin.

Using an electric mixer, beat the butter and sugar together until light and fluffy. Add the eggs a little at a time, beating well after each addition. Mix in the marmalade. Sift the flour, baking powder, spice and ground almonds together and fold them into the mixture using a large metal spoon. Fold in the fruit and any whisky that has not been absorbed.

Spoon the mixture into the prepared cake tin, level the top with a spatula and decorate with the blanched almonds. Bake for 45 minutes, then check that the top is not getting too dark; cover it with foil if necessary. Bake for a further 30 minutes, until the cake is firm to the touch and a skewer inserted in the centre comes out clean. Leave to cool in the tin.

20

Dutch Apple Cake
Holland

A recipe for apple cake features in a Dutch cookbook dating from 1514. It is not dissimilar to today's recipes. Cinnamon and raisins or sultanas usually feature, along with some kind of icing. The cakes tend to be baked in shallow tins to resemble tarts and have a topping of sharp, crisp apples, sliced into neat wedges.

This recipe makes a wonderful dessert, served warm with a dollop of ice cream or Chantilly cream.

Makes a 25cm cake

2 large eggs
1 teaspoon vanilla extract
175g light soft brown sugar
85g unsalted butter
125g plain flour
1 teaspoon ground cinnamon
½ teaspoon baking powder
50g sultanas
25ml milk
4 small dessert apples, peeled, cored and thinly sliced
1 tablespoon demerara sugar

Icing
4 tablespoons icing sugar
1–2 tablespoons Calvados or brandy

To decorate
75g flaked almonds, toasted
a little icing sugar

Preheat the oven to 170°C/ Gas Mark 3. Grease and line a 25cm square shallow cake tin.

Place the eggs, vanilla extract and sugar in a bowl and whisk with an electric mixer on medium to high speed for about 5 minutes, until the mixture is pale, has increased in volume and is thick enough to leave a trail when dropped from the whisk.

Gently melt the butter in a small pan. Using a large metal spoon, fold it into the whisked batter, taking care not to lose volume. Sift the flour, cinnamon and baking powder together and add the sultanas. Mix to coat the sultanas – this will help prevent them sinking to the bottom of the cake. Fold into the whisked mixture 2 tablespoons at a time, then fold in the milk. Transfer the mixture to the prepared tin. Arrange the apple slices on top and sprinkle with the demerara sugar. Bake for 20–25 minutes, until the sponge is golden brown and the apples are lightly coloured. Remove from the oven and leave to cool in the tin.

Whisk the icing sugar with enough Calvados or brandy to form a translucent icing. Brush it over the cake while it is still warm. Arrange the flaked almonds around the edge of the cake and dust with a little icing sugar.

21

Austrian Coffee Cake
Austria

When the Turkish army retreated in haste after the Battle of Vienna in 1683, they left behind bags of coffee, or so the story goes. Perhaps it was the bountiful supply of coffee that led to Vienna's famous café culture. Many a fine cake has come out of Vienna and this coffee cake is a prime example of how good a sponge cake can be. It is really simple to make but the results are stunning. I was reminded of this when I went for dinner at my neighbour's house. Kath baked this cake for dessert and filled it with fresh raspberries.
Use whatever fruits are in season.

Makes a 20cm cake

185g unsalted butter, at room
   temperature
185g caster sugar
3 medium eggs, lightly beaten
185g self-raising flour, sifted
a pinch of salt

To finish
125g hot, strong black coffee
15g caster sugar
1 tablespoon rum
300ml whipping cream
25g icing sugar
½ teaspoon vanilla extract

To decorate
1 tube (2g) freeze-dried raspberries
5 fresh black figs
5g candied rose fragments

Heat the oven to 170°C/Gas Mark
3. Grease and flour a 20cm bundt
ring tin. Using an electric mixer, beat
the butter and sugar together until
light and fluffy. Gradually beat in the
eggs, creaming well after each
addition. Fold in the flour and salt
with a large metal spoon.

Transfer the mixture to the
prepared cake tin and bake for
about 25 minutes, until it is golden
brown and springs back when gently
pressed with your finger. Leave in the
tin for 10 minutes, then turn out on
to a wire rack to cool.

Sweeten the hot coffee with the
sugar and stir in the rum. Return the
cooled cake to the bundt tin and
slowly pour the coffee over it. Invert
immediately on to a serving plate
and leave to cool once more.

Put the cream in a bowl with the
icing sugar and vanilla and whip to
medium peaks. Spread most of it
over the cake, using a palette knife;
it does not have to look perfectly
smooth. Spoon or pipe the remaining
cream into the centre of the cake and
level with a spatula. Grind half the
freeze-dried raspberries to a powder
in a pestle and mortar or with a
spice grinder. Using a tea strainer,
dust the powder over the cream.
Sprinkle with the remaining
raspberry pieces. Cut the figs into
quarters and arrange them in a
circular fashion on top of the cake.
Sprinkle with the candied rose
fragments.

22

Genoa Cake
Italy

It seems the UK coined the name for this light, citrus-flavoured fruitcake, which is a variation on the pandolce *cake from Genoa in Italy. The original contained cherries, sultanas, pine nuts, dried fruits, candied orange peel and almonds, and was made with yeast rather than baking powder. Fruitcakes are my all-time favourite cakes, so the Genoa cake is right up there in my top ten. This recipe is very easy to make, and really good if you don't like your fruitcake too heavy. Try it buttered, too.*

Makes a small loaf

125g unsalted butter
125g golden caster sugar
3 medium eggs, lightly beaten
1 teaspoon vanilla extract
grated zest of ½ lemon
grated zest of 1 orange
50g natural-dye red glacé cherries, halved
50g green glacé cherries, left whole
50g bright-red glacé cherries left whole
50g mixed candied peel, chopped
150g sultanas
150g dried apricots, chopped
25g whole blanched almonds
115g plain flour
60g self-raising flour
1 teaspoon ground mixed spice
60ml Cointreau or brandy

Topping
100g apricot jam
50g whole blanched almonds
50–70g glacé cherries

Heat the oven to 150°C/Gas Mark 2. Grease a 450g loaf tin and line the base and long sides with a piece of baking parchment.

Using an electric mixer, beat the butter and sugar together until pale and fluffy. Add the eggs a little at a time, beating well after each addition. Mix in the vanilla extract and lemon and orange zest. In a separate bowl, mix the fruit and nuts with a tablespoon of the plain flour until well coated; this will help prevent them sinking in the cake. Sift the remaining plain flour with the self-raising flour and mixed spice and fold into the batter with a large metal spoon. Carefully fold in the dried fruits, taking care not to over mix. Spoon into the prepared tin and level the top.

Bake for 55 minutes, until the cake is springy to the touch and a skewer inserted in the centre comes out clean. Pierce the cake several times with a skewer and pour over the Cointreau or brandy. Leave to cool in the tin. Warm the apricot jam in a small pan and brush it over the top of the cake. Decorate with the whole almonds and glacé cherries.

23

Walnut Cake
Greece

Walnuts are plentiful in Greece and have been used in cooking since ancient times, with walnut cake, or karythopita, *being especially popular. In the past, many cakes were unleavened and, for this reason, they were often soaked immediately after baking to soften them. The red wine in this recipe is my addition. It adds a kick to the cake that complements the spices.*

Makes 8–12 individual cakes or one 23cm cake

20g ground semolina
1 teaspoon ground cinnamon
½ teaspoon ground mixed spice
35g white breadcrumbs
150g walnuts, finely ground
5 large eggs, separated
90g caster sugar
2 tablespoons red wine
juice and grated zest of 1 orange

Spice syrup
250g caster sugar
150ml water
150ml red wine
6 cloves
1 cinnamon stick
juice and grated zest of 1 lemon
50g walnuts, chopped

Heat the oven to 170°C/Gas Mark 3. Grease and flour 8–12 individual oblong cake tins or a 23cm round deep tin.

Place the semolina, cinnamon, mixed spice, breadcrumbs and ground walnuts in a bowl and mix well. Using an electric mixer, whisk together the egg yolks, sugar, red wine, orange juice and zest until smooth, creamy and pale in colour. In a separate bowl, whisk the egg whites to stiff peaks. Fold the dried ingredients into the egg yolk mixture, then carefully fold in the egg whites, using a large metal spoon.

Spoon the mixture into the prepared tins and bake for 18–20 minutes for individual cakes, 35–40 minutes for a large one. When the cake is done, it should spring back when pressed gently with your finger and a skewer inserted in the centre should come out clean.

Meanwhile, make the spice syrup. Put all the ingredients except the walnuts into a small saucepan and bring to the boil, stirring. Simmer for 5 minutes, then remove from the heat and strain through a sieve into a jug. Return half the syrup to the pan and simmer until reduced to a thick coating consistency.

When the cakes are ready, remove them from the oven and pour over the syrup from the jug. Leave to cool for 15 minutes, then remove the cakes from the tins. Add the chopped walnuts to the reduced syrup and drizzle it over the cakes. They are really good with a dollop of whipped cream flavoured with vanilla.

24 Green Tea Roulade
Japan

I recently spent some time in Japan, visiting Osaka, Tokyo and Kyoto. Most traditional Japanese cakes are made using bean paste and crafted by experts rather than baked at home. However, I did see many cakes made with matcha tea – hence the inspiration for this roulade.

I was given the colourful sugar pieces used to decorate the cake in the photo by Nita Sun, a pastry chef at the Ritz Carlton Hotel in Osaka. He comes from Kyoto, where these sugar pieces are given to children as a treat. I spun my roulade with white chocolate, so you don't really need the sugar too, unless you happen to have it.

3 tablespoons green tea powder
3 tablespoons hot water
90g plain flour
25g cornflour
8 egg yolks
160g caster sugar, plus extra for dusting
6 egg whites
50ml vegetable oil

Filling
300ml whipping cream
25g icing sugar, sifted
1 teaspoon vanilla extract

To decorate
50g white chocolate

Heat the oven to 200°C/Gas Mark 6. Grease a 35cm x 28cm Swiss roll tin and line with baking parchment.

Dissolve the green tea powder in the hot water and leave to cool. Sift the flour and cornflour together and set aside. Using an electric beater, whisk the egg yolks with 100g of the sugar until thick and pale. Add the green tea mixture and whisk to combine. In a separate bowl, whisk the egg whites and the remaining sugar to stiff peaks. Using a large metal spoon, fold the egg whites into the egg yolk mixture a third at a time. Sprinkle a third of the sifted flour over the surface and fold it in. Repeat until all the flour has been added, taking care not to over mix and lose volume. Finally, fold in the oil.

Pour the batter into the prepared tin and level the surface with a palette knife. Bake for 10–15 minutes, until the cake springs back when gently pressed with your finger. Do not over cook or the cake will be difficult to roll. Remove from the oven and transfer the sponge, still on the paper, to a work surface. Place another piece of paper on top of the sponge and roll it up lightly. This will help to make it easier to roll later. Leave to cool.

To make the filling, whisk the cream with the icing sugar and vanilla until it just holds it shape.

To assemble, unroll the cake on a piece of baking parchment lightly dusted with caster sugar; it should be slightly bigger than the sponge. Carefully peel off the backing paper. Spread the cream evenly over the cake. With a long side nearest you, turn over 1–2cm of the cake to start the formation of the roll. Now work along the length of the roll, keeping it tight, and begin to roll the sponge up. Once you are half way it will become easier.

Melt the white chocolate in a microwave or in a small bowl set over a pan of gently simmering water, making sure the water doesn't touch the base of the bowl. Put it in a disposable piping bag, snip a small amount off the tip and zigzag the chocolate back and forth over the cake. Refrigerate for 30 minutes, then trim the ends off the roulade to neaten. It is best eaten on the day of making.

25 Fondant Fancies
England

Is there anyone in the UK who has not enjoyed a Mr Kipling cake during childhood? Mr Kipling, he of 'exceedingly good cake' fame, was a fictional creation – invented as a brand for a mass cake manufacturer at a time when we still bought 90 per cent of our cakes from high-street bakers. So popular were the adverts, and the little squares of pink, yellow and brown fondant cake, that the brand has remained market leader for over 30 years. That's some achievement, and a testament to our love of fondant fancies and other sweet delights. I have made mine a less than traditional assortment of vibrantly coloured sponge cubes.

Makes 20

175g unsalted butter, softened
150g caster sugar
4 small eggs
1 teaspoon vanilla extract
25g plain flour
25g cornflour
175g ground almonds

Orange syrup
75g caster sugar
75ml water
a few drops of orange oil

Buttercream
100g unsalted butter, softened
140g icing sugar
1 teaspoon vanilla extract

To finish
a little icing sugar
250g white marzipan
500–700g soft confectioner's
    fondant (see page 188)
yellow, orange, pink and blue gel food colourings
polka dot and chocolate bean
    sprinkles

Heat the oven to 170°C/Gas Mark 3. Grease a 20cm square, shallow cake tin and line the base with baking parchment.

Cream the butter and sugar together until pale and fluffy. Lightly beat the eggs with the vanilla, then add them a little at a time, beating well after each addition. Sift the flour and cornflour together and mix with the ground almonds, making sure there are no lumps. Fold the dry ingredients into the cake mixture, being careful not to over mix. Transfer to the prepared tin and level the top with a spatula. Bake for about 25 minutes, until the cake is golden brown and springs back when pressed lightly with your finger. Leave to cool in the tin.

To make the syrup, put the sugar and water in a small pan and bring to the boil. Remove from the heat and add the orange oil. Cut the cake horizontally in half and brush the cut surface with the warm orange syrup.

To make the buttercream, beat the butter and icing sugar together with an electric mixer on medium speed until very light and fluffy. Mix in the vanilla. Sandwich the cake halves together with most of the buttercream and leave in the fridge for 30 minutes to firm up.

On a surface lightly dusted with icing sugar, roll the marzipan out into a square large enough to cover the cake. Spread the top of the cake with a little buttercream and level it with a spatula. Lay the marzipan on top, trimming off the excess. Flip the cake over on to a chopping board dusted lightly with icing sugar, so the marzipan is underneath. Cut the cake into 4cm cubes and set them right-side up, 2–3cm apart on a wire rack. Rest the rack over a tray to catch the excess fondant.

Put half the fondant in a pan with 2 tablespoons of water and heat gently to no more than blood heat (37°C); you could also do this carefully in a microwave. If the fondant gets too hot, it will go dull and crack when it is set. Mix in a little yellow food colouring. Using a tablespoon, pour the fondant over 5 of the cakes, making sure it runs down the sides. It's easiest if you put plenty on your spoon to begin with. Work with one colour at a time and once you have finished with that colour, remove the rack from over the tray and scape the fondant that has run off the cakes back into the pan. Add some orange colouring to the remaining yellow fondant and use to ice 5 more cakes. Warm the second half of the fondant with 2 tablespoons of water, colour it pink and repeat the process with 5 more cakes. Finally, colour the remaining pink fondant blue and use to ice the remaining cakes. If you want more vibrant colours, divide the fondant into 4 and colour each batch separately. Bear in mind that it is harder to work with a small amount of fondant.

Use a little knife dipped in hot water to cut the cakes from the rack. Place them into round cake cases, pressing the sides gently so they take the shape of the cake. Decorate with the sprinkles. The cakes will keep in a tin for 3–4 days.

26 Guinness and Chocolate Cupcakes
Ireland

The traditional burnt flavour of Guinness comes from roasted unmalted barley. My father used to drink in his local pub with the late Sir Peter Guinness, a descendant of the founder, Arthur Guinness, who had his own 'special' barrel of Guinness shipped in from Ireland. Even though Guinness is now produced all over the world, it is still brewed differently in Ireland.

It takes a lot of black colouring to make the frosting for these cupcakes truly black; I stopped at one tube, when the colour was still more grey than black. If you want a really good dark shade, it's worth trying to find a particularly concentrated colouring, as using too much will make the frosting too soft.

Makes 10

40g cocoa powder
170g unsalted butter
1 teaspoon vanilla extract
1 large egg
125ml Guinness
70g plain flour
½ teaspoon bicarbonate of soda
170g caster sugar

Frosting
165g unsalted butter
250g icing sugar, sifted
1–2 tablespoons Baileys Irish Cream, to taste
½–1 tube of black food colouring

To decorate
silver balls
silver shimmer spray

Heat the oven to 170°C/Gas Mark 3. Put 10 cupcake cases in muffin tins.

Sift the cocoa powder into a bowl. Melt the butter in a small pan and pour it into the cocoa powder. Add the vanilla extract, egg and Guinness and whisk to combine.

Sift the flour, bicarbonate of soda and sugar together into a large mixing bowl and make a well in the centre. Pour in the Guinness mix and whisk to a smooth, shiny batter. Spoon or pipe into the cupcake cases, filling them two-thirds full. Bake for 17–20 minutes, until the tops spring back when pressed lightly with your finger and a skewer inserted in the centre comes out clean. Leave to cool on a wire rack.

Meanwhile, make the frosting. Using an electric mixer on high speed, beat the butter and sugar together until light and fluffy. Add the Baileys and whisk for 5 minutes, until the frosting becomes paler. Divide the frosting between 2 bowls and add enough food colouring to one portion to colour it black – or as dark as possible.

Fit a piping bag with a plain 1cm nozzle and spoon both frostings into it, trying to arrange them side by side in the bag so they both come out together. Pipe a large swirl of the frosting on top of each cupcake. Sprinkle with a few silver balls and spray with shimmer spray.

27

Mil Hojas
Chile

This is the Chilean version of a millefeuille, or thousand leaves. In Chile it is sandwiched together with dulce de leche. I have made it a little more like the French millefeuille here by using a pastry cream flavoured with dulce de leche as well as the straight-up milky caramel. Walnuts add crunch and extra flavour to the buttery pastry and caramel.

This is best eaten on the day it is made, as the filling will cause the pastry to soften. It's perfectly okay to make the pastry layers one day and fill them the next. Just put them back into the oven for 10 minutes to refresh them before cooling and filling.

Makes an 18cm cake

320g ready-rolled all-butter puff
    pastry
440ml dulce de leche
2 tablespoons brandy
200g walnuts, toasted and finely
    chopped
2 tablespoons icing sugar

Pastry cream
2 medium eggs
125g caster sugar
15g plain flour
15g cornflour
½ vanilla pod
250ml milk

Start by making the pastry cream. Put the eggs and sugar into a bowl, sift in the flour and cornflour and mix to a smooth paste. Slit the vanilla pod open lengthwise, put it in a pan with the milk and bring to the boil. Gradually pour the hot milk on to the egg mix, whisking to combine. Remove the vanilla pod and scrape the seeds into the mix. Return the mixture to the pan and cook over a moderate heat, whisking continuously, until it thickens and comes to the boil. Reduce the heat and continue whisking for a minute longer. Transfer to a clean container and cover the surface with cling film to prevent a skin forming. Leave to cool.

Heat the oven to 180°C/Gas Mark 4. Cut the pastry into circles using an 18cm cutter – or you can use a plate turned upside down as a guide to cut around. Place the discs on non-stick baking trays, setting them slightly apart. Re-roll any trimmings and cut out as many discs as you can; you should end up with 3 or 4. Bake for 20–25 minutes, until golden brown and crisp, checking that the base of the pastry is also coloured. Leave to cool on the trays.

Scoop the dulce de leche from the jar into a bowl and whisk gently until it is smooth. Mix in the brandy. Whisk the cooled pastry cream to loosen it and then gently stir in 2 tablespoons of the dulce de leche.

Take a large serrated bread knife and cut each disc horizontally in half to make 2 thinner discs. Take care, as they will be fragile. Assemble the cake on a cake board or plate, as it will be hard to transfer once you have finished. Take the first layer of pastry and spread it with a layer of the pastry cream about 5mm thick. Place the next layer of pastry on top, spread with dulce de leche and sprinkle with some chopped walnuts. Repeat this process until you have used up all the ingredients Sift the icing sugar over the top and sprinkle with any remaining chopped walnuts.

28 Pineapple Cakes
Taiwan

These little cakes are really more like pies. The filling is generally quite sweet but many bakers add melon to make it less so. Pineapple cakes can be bought on every street corner in Taiwan and they are very popular – so much so that producer Vigor Kobo once sold 100,000 of its much sought-after pineapple cakes in a single day. That's a lot of cakes. Perhaps their popularity is due to the fact that the pineapple symbolises wealth.

When I first made these, I scoffed two straight out of the oven, burning my mouth in the process. Despite that, I love them and will certainly be making them again and again.

Makes 12

330g plain flour
2 tablespoons cornflour
2 tablespoons milk powder
230g unsalted butter
20g vegetable shortening or lard
30g icing sugar, plus extra for dusting
1 medium egg
½ teaspoon vanilla extract

Pineapple filling
375g fresh pineapple, diced
750g honeydew melon, diced
170g caster sugar
3 tablespoons golden syrup

To make the pastry sift the flour, cornflour and milk powder together. Using an electric mixer with the paddle attachment, cream the butter, shortening or lard and icing sugar together for about 8 minutes, until very light and fluffy. Mix in the egg and vanilla extract. On a very low speed, mix in the flour, cornflour and milk powder, being careful not to overwork the mixture. Wrap in cling film and refrigerate for 1 hour.

To make the filling, place the pineapple and melon in a food processor or blender and pulse until puréed. Place in a heavy-based pan and cook over a medium heat, stirring occasionally, for 20 minutes, until most of the liquid has evaporated. Stir in the sugar, and cook for about 8 minutes, until thickened. Stir in the golden syrup and cook, stirring constantly, for 10–12 minutes, until the mixture is very thick, sticky and uniformly light amber in colour. Remove from the heat and leave to cool.

Heat the oven to 170°C/Gas Mark 3. Lightly grease a non-stick cake tray with 12 rectangular holes. Divide the dough into 12 pieces and roll each one out on a lightly floured surface into a round approximately 10cm in diameter. Press into the tins to line, then cut away the excess. Place a large spoonful of the filling in each one. Re-roll the pastry trimmings and cut out pieces to cover the tops of the pies. Brush around the top of the filled pies with a little water and put the pastry lids on top, pressing them down gently so they stick to the edges.

Bake for 25–30 minutes, until the pastry is golden brown. Eat warm, but take care, as the filling will be piping hot. They are also very good cold. The best way to get them out of the tray is to turn it over on to a work surface and give it a gentle tap and they will come tumbling out. Dust with a little icing sugar before serving.

29

Nata Cake
Cuba

This is a traditional Cuban cream cake used to celebrate special occasions. It is soaked in condensed and evaporated milk, then covered in whipped cream. Although it's not traditional, I like to jazz mine up with cubes of fresh pineapple and mango. I adapted this recipe from cookery writers and broadcasters, Three Guys from Miami, because I love the combination of mango, coconut and rum. Thanks, guys.

Makes a 20cm cake

210g self-raising flour
½ teaspoon salt
325ml whipping cream
3 medium eggs
335g caster sugar
1 teaspoon vanilla extract

Filling
1 ripe mango
375ml condensed milk
410ml evaporated milk
3 egg yolks
30g cornflour
1 teaspoon vanilla extract
200ml coconut milk
25ml white rum (optional)

To decorate
300ml whipping cream
100g toasted coconut
¼ pineapple, peeled, cored and cut
    into cubes (or a small can of
    pineapple chunks)
1 ripe mango, peeled, stoned and cut
    into 2.5cm cubes

Heat the oven to 170°C/Gas Mark 3. Grease and flour a 20cm springform cake tin.

Sift the flour and salt into a large bowl. Whisk the cream until it holds soft peaks and then place in the fridge. Using an electric mixer, whisk the eggs, sugar and vanilla together until light, fluffy and tripled in volume. Fold the cream into the whisked egg mixture with a large metal spoon, then fold in the flour a little at a time, taking care not to lose the volume. The mixture will be quite thick. Transfer to the prepared cake tin and bake for 25–30 minutes, until golden brown. The top should spring back when pressed gently with your finger. Cool in the tin for 10 minutes, then turn out on to a wire rack to cool completely.

Meanwhile, make the filling. Peel and stone the mango, then purée the flesh in a blender or food processor. Transfer to a pan, add the condensed milk and evaporated milk and bring slowly to the boil. Whisk the egg yolks with the cornflour and vanilla to make a smooth paste. Pour the boiled mixture over the egg yolks, whisking to combine. Return to the pan and bring back to the boil, whisking constantly until thickened. Pour into a clean bowl, cover the surface with cling film and leave to cool, then chill.

Mix the coconut milk with the rum, if using. Cut the cake horizontally into 3 layers. Place the top layer cut-side up on a cake card and, using a pastry brush, soak it with the coconut milk.

Remove the filling from the fridge and whisk gently to soften. Spread the cake with about a third of the filling. Put the middle layer of sponge on top, soak with the coconut milk and spread with another third of the filling. Place the bottom layer of cake on top and press down lightly to level, then brush with the coconut milk. Now place the cake in the fridge for 30 minutes to firm up.

Mix the remaining filling with the whipping cream and whisk until it holds its shape. Spoon a big dollop of the cream on top of the cake and make a well in the centre with the back of the spoon. Coat the sides of the cake with the remaining cream, using a palette knife or spatula. Press the toasted coconut around the sides of the cake. Place the prepared fruit in the well in the cream.

30

Pink Lamingtons
Australia

Pretty as a picture, these pink cakes originate from Australia. There is some controversy about their origins. Some say they were named after Baron Lamington, the Governor of Queensland from 1895 to 1901. Others think that Lady Lamington, patron of a famous cooking school in Brisbane, was so admired that the cookery teacher, Amy Shauer, named them after her. I like this version of events, as Baron Lamington didn't even like cake and was apparently a rather grumpy man.

Traditionally the cakes are chocolate and coconut, filled with a layer of plum jam, but I love this pink version and they can be adapted to several flavours. I have used raspberry jam here but strawberry, redcurrant and, of course, plum all work a treat. For extra texture, these are filled with fresh cream too.

Makes 12

250g unsalted butter, at room temperature
300g caster sugar
4 medium eggs, lightly beaten
½ teaspoon vanilla extract
500g self-raising flour
a pinch of salt
250ml milk

Icing and coating
385g icing sugar
125ml milk
20g unsalted butter, finely diced
a little pink food colouring
250g shredded coconut

Filling
250ml double cream
15g icing sugar
½ teaspoon vanilla extract
4 tablespoons raspberry jam

Heat the oven to 170°C/Gas Mark 3. Grease a 17cm x 27cm baking tin, 3cm deep, and line the base with baking parchment.

Using an electric mixer, cream the butter and sugar together until pale and fluffy. Add the eggs a little at a time, beating well after each addition, then mix in the vanilla extract. Sift the flour and salt together. Fold them in alternately with the milk, starting and finishing with the flour. Take care not to over mix the batter. Transfer the mixture to the prepared cake tin and level the surface with a palette knife.

Bake for 30–35 minutes, until the cake is well risen and golden and springs back when lightly pressed with your finger. Leave to cool in the tin, then remove from the tin and leave in the fridge for 1 hour to firm up.

Using a long, serrated knife, cut the sponge into 12 equal pieces. Sift the icing sugar into a heatproof bowl. Gradually add the milk, whisking to keep the mixture smooth, then add the butter. Place the bowl over a pan of gently simmering water, making sure the water doesn't touch the base of the bowl. Stir continuously for 3–4 minutes, until the icing is hot. Remove from the heat and stir in a little pink colouring.

Put the shredded coconut in a bowl. One at a time, dip each lamington into the icing, using a fish slice or spatula to lift them out. Make sure the excess icing has drained off back into the bowl of icing, then put the lamington in the coconut and roll to coat. Lift on to a tray lined with baking parchment and leave for 2 hours to firm and set.

To make the filling, put the double cream, icing sugar and vanilla in a bowl and whisk to medium peaks. It should be thick enough to spread.

Split each cake in half and sandwich together with the raspberry jam and whipped cream. Once filled, eat within 3 days. The unfilled cakes can be frozen for 3 months.

31 Pineapple Rum Cake
Martinique

Martinique is not short of pineapples and rum, and both feature in almost all its cakes and desserts. Martinique rums are some of the best in the world, and it is not considered an extravagance to include them in sweet dishes. Many of the recipes are similar to pineapple upside-down cakes but I liked this one the best, as the cake is really moist and well flavoured. I have jazzed it up with yellow buttercream. If you have limited time, cut out the fancy decorating part and simply rough ice the cake with the buttercream, sprinkling the decorations on top. It will still taste amazing.

You can bake this in a deep 23cm cake tin but, since the cake is so moist, it may be quite tricky to cut. I used three sandwich cake tins; if you only have two, bake two layers then re-line one tin and bake the third separately.

Makes a 23cm cake

435g can of pineapple rings
330g plain flour
½ teaspoon salt
20g baking powder
500ml whipping cream
4 medium eggs
1 teaspoon vanilla extract
450g caster sugar

Rum syrup

200g caster sugar
50ml white rum

Buttercream

300g caster sugar
100ml water
5 medium egg whites
500g softened unsalted butter, cut

into 2.5cm cubes
a little yellow food colouring
½ teaspoon vanilla extract

To decorate

50g white chocolate, grated
20g candied pineapple cubes, chopped
pearl sugar dragees

Heat the oven to 170°C/Gas Mark 3. Grease three 23cm sandwich cake tins, line the bases with baking parchment, then flour the sides of the tins.

Drain the pineapple, reserving the juice, then cut it into 5mm dice. Sift the flour, salt and baking powder together 3 times and set aside. Using an electric mixer, whisk the cream to soft peaks. Add the eggs, vanilla and sugar and whisk until thick, pale and trebled in volume. Fold in the chopped pineapple with a large metal spoon, then fold in the flour mixture.

Divide the mixture between the prepared cake tins and bake for 25–30 minutes, until the top springs back when pressed gently with your finger and a skewer inserted in the centre comes out clean. Leave to cool in the tins for 10 minutes, then turn out on to a wire rack to cool completely.

For the rum syrup, take 200ml of the reserved pineapple juice and make it up to 250ml with water. Pour into a pan, add the sugar and bring to the boil, stirring to dissolve the sugar. Remove from the heat and stir in the rum, then leave to cool.

To make the buttercream, put 250g of the sugar in a deep, heavy-based pan with the water and wash

down the sides of the pan with a pastry brush dipped in cold water to remove any sugar crystals. Place a sugar thermometer in the pan and then bring to the boil, without stirring, over a high heat. Cook until the sugar thermometer registers 118°C. Meanwhile, place the egg whites in a freestanding electric mixer with the remaining sugar and whisk on medium speed. As soon as the sugar syrup reaches the correct temperature, remove from the heat and pour in a slow trickle on to the egg whites, whisking on low speed. Once all the syrup has been added, turn up the speed and continue to whisk until the meringue is thick and has cooled to hand hot. Reduce the speed to low and add the soft butter a cube or two at a time, still whisking, to make a smooth, silky buttercream. Finally mix in a few drops of yellow food colouring and the vanilla.

To assemble the cake, place one of the sponge layers on a cake card and soak it well with the rum syrup, using a pastry brush. Spread with a 5mm-thick layer of the buttercream, then place a second layer of sponge on top, soak it with the rum syrup and spread with another 5mm-thick layer of buttercream. Soak the final layer of sponge with syrup, put it on top of the cake and press down gently to level it. Coat the outside of the cake thinly with buttercream, using a palette knife. Chill the cake for at least 20 minutes, until the buttercream is firm.

The next layer of buttercream will be the final coating and should look as neat as possible. Coat the cake with a thicker layer of buttercream,

putting two-thirds of it on top of the cake and smoothing it over to the sides. Use a palette knife that is longer than the width of the cake, holding it at a slight 45-degree angle and running it back and forth over the cake to give a smooth top. The buttercream will fall on to the sides of the cake; this is perfectly

normal. Now pick the cake up on its cake card and support it with the palm of your hand. Place the bottom of the palette knife up against the side of the cake so it is parallel to the cake and pull it downwards in short strokes to remove excess buttercream neatly. Work your way around the entire cake.

Coat the sides of the cake with the grated white chocolate and chopped candied pineapple cubes. Mark the top of the cake in a criss-cross fashion with a long knife, then place a pearl dragee at the centre of each cross. Put your feet up and enjoy with a rum cocktail – you deserve it.

32 Macaroons
France

Macaroons can be tricky to get right and might take a few attempts to master, but once you get the hang of them you will soon be creating your own flavours. Lakeland stocks an inspirational array of flavour drops, from popcorn to lavender. Here I've chosen to fill the macaroons with a lavender buttercream and an orange and lemon curd, but anything goes.

I prefer to use paste rather than liquid colourings for macaroons, as you need add only a very small amount and they give more vibrant colours.

Makes 40

125g ground almonds
225g icing sugar
4 medium egg whites
a pinch of cream of tartar
25g caster sugar
a little purple food colouring
a little orange food colouring

St Clements curd
2 large eggs
75g caster sugar
75g unsalted butter, diced
juice and grated zest of 1 lemon
juice and grated zest of 1 orange

Lavender buttercream
150g caster sugar
50ml water
2 egg whites
250g soft unsalted butter, diced
a little purple food colouring
2 drops of lavender extract

Heat the oven to 180°C/Gas Mark 4. Sift the ground almonds and icing sugar together on to a piece of baking parchment, then sift again. If you have a food processor or small grinder, you can grind them together for 30 seconds and then sift them. Divide the mixture in half, weighing it out carefully.

Using an electric mixer, whisk the egg whites until they are just foamy, then add the cream of tartar and whisk to soft peaks. Reduce the speed and add the caster sugar, then return to a high speed and whisk until the meringue is firm. Transfer half the mixture to a bowl and whisk in one of the food colourings until well blended. Whisk the second food colouring into the remaining meringue. Fold half the dry ingredients into each portion of meringue until the mixture is smooth and shiny but still holds its shape.

Using a piping bag fitted with a 1cm nozzle, pipe each mixture on to a baking sheet lined with a silicone baking mat. The macaroons should be about 2cm in diameter, with 2.5cm between each one. Tap the tray on the work surface to flatten the mixture slightly. Leave the macaroons for about 15 minutes to form a skin, then bake in the centre of the oven for 10 minutes, leaving the oven door very slightly ajar to let the steam escape. They should rise from the bases a little and be crisp and firm on top. As soon as you remove them from the oven, run a little cold water between the baking parchment and the baking tray; this will make it easier to remove the macaroons from the paper. Allow 2–3 minutes for them to cool before lifting them off the baking parchment. Leave until completely cold.

To make the St Clements curd, place all the ingredients in a bowl set over a pan of simmering water, making sure the water doesn't touch the base of the bowl. Whisk gently with a hand whisk until the curd thickens enough to leave a trail on the surface; this can take 10–15 minutes. If you have a blender, pour the hot curd into it as soon as it thickens and blitz on high for 1–2 minutes to lighten it. Pour into a bowl, cover the surface with cling film and leave to cool.

To make the buttercream, put 125g of the sugar in a deep, heavy-based pan with the water and wash down the sides of the pan with a pastry brush dipped in cold water to remove any sugar crystals. Place a sugar thermometer in the pan and then bring to the boil, without stirring, over a high heat. Cook until the sugar thermometer registers 118°C. Meanwhile, place the egg whites in a freestanding electric mixer with the remaining sugar and whisk on medium speed. As soon as the sugar syrup reaches the correct temperature, remove from the heat and pour in a slow trickle on to the egg whites, whisking on low speed. Once all the syrup has been added, turn up the speed and continue to whisk until the meringue is thick and has cooled to hand hot. Reduce the speed to low and add the soft butter a cube or two at a time, still whisking, to make a smooth, silky buttercream. Finally mix in the food colouring and lavender extract.

Put each filling into a piping bag fitted with a 5mm plain nozzle. Sandwich the purple macaroons together with the lavender buttercream and the orange macaroons with the curd.

33 Tres Leches Cake
Mexico

Tres leches *means three milks, and this cake is soaked in a lavish mixture of double cream, evaporated milk and condensed milk. I'm sure we can thank Nestlé, who used to have condensed milk factories across South America, for its popularity. I have made it several times and it's always a winner, devoured in minutes. The combination of light, fluffy sponge soaked with the sweet milk, plus lashings of caramel and cream, is a great idea. The diet starts tomorrow.*

Makes a 23cm cake

6 large eggs, separated
450g caster sugar
2 teaspoons vanilla extract
235g plain flour
2 teaspoons baking powder
125ml whole milk

Three milks
300ml double cream
440ml evaporated milk
440ml condensed milk

Filling
300ml whipping cream
440ml dulce de leche

To decorate
500ml whipping cream
1 teaspoon vanilla extract
25g icing sugar
30g flaked almonds, toasted and
  chopped
4–6 wafer butterflies (optional)

Heat the oven to 170°C/Gas Mark 3. Grease a 23cm round cake tin and line the base with baking parchment. Grease again and dust with flour.

Put the egg whites and half the sugar in a freestanding electric mixer fitted with a whisk attachment and beat on medium speed until soft peaks form. Reduce the speed to low and gradually add the remaining sugar, beating to stiff peaks; this should take 3–4 minutes. Add the egg yolks, one at a time, while mixing on a low speed to incorporate. Mix in the vanilla. Sift the flour and baking powder together. Using a large spoon, fold the flour into the mixture in stages, alternating with the whole milk and beginning and ending with flour. Take care so the mixture does not lose its volume.

Transfer the mixture to the prepared tin and bake for 30–35 minutes, until the cake is golden brown and springs back when pressed lightly with your finger; a skewer inserted in the centre should come out clean. Remove the cake from the oven and leave in the tin for 5 minutes, before turning out on to a wire rack to cool.

For the three milks, place the cream and evaporated milk in a pan and bring to the boil, stirring to prevent it catching on the bottom of the pan. Stir in the condensed milk, remove from the heat and leave to cool.

Whisk the cream for the filling to firm peaks and place in the fridge. Put the dulce de leche in a bowl and stir until it is soft and spreadable.

Turn the cake over so the bottom is now the top. Cut it horizontally into 3 even layers. Place the bottom

layer on a cake card and soak well with the three milks, applying them with a pastry brush; the cake should feel squidgy and soft. Spread with a layer of dulce de leche, then spread with half the whipped cream and level the top. Place the next layer of sponge cake on top, soak well with the milks and repeat the layers as before. Turn the top cake layer over and soak the cut side with a little of the milk mixture, taking care that you can still pick it up. Turn it over on to the top of the cake and press down to level. Cover the cake and chill for at least 4 hours or overnight. Reserve any remaining milk mixture in the fridge.

Whisk the cream and vanilla for the decoration to firm peaks. Using a palette knife, coat the sides of the cake with a thin layer of the whipped cream to seal and make a smooth surface. Spread a thicker layer on the top and rough it up a little to create waves. Clean any excess cream from the sides of the cake with a palette knife so it looks neat.

Place the remaining cream in a piping bag fitted with a large leaf nozzle. Starting at the bottom of the cake, pipe a row of leaves around the edge – to do this, place the piping nozzle up to the side of the cake and gently squeeze it until it makes a short leaf. Stop and make another one directly next to it, then continue all the way around the cake. Once you have completed that row, start another row above it and repeat until you reach the top of the cake. Dust the top with the icing sugar.

Press the chopped almonds around the sides of the cake, just covering

about 5cm around the base.
Decorate the top with the wafer
butterflies, if using.

Serve cut into slices, with any
remaining milk mixture poured over
the top.

34

Basbousa
Egypt

My dear friend Firas shared his mother's recipe for this simple, tasty cake with me. The addition of coconut is not traditional but I love the softer texture it creates. Once the cake has been baked, it is soaked in a beautiful rose syrup. I make mine in individual card loaf cases but traditionally it is baked in a large tin.

Makes 15–20 mini cakes or one 23cm x 33cm cake

250g coarse semolina
250g fine semolina
225g caster sugar
100g desiccated coconut
2 teaspoons baking powder
225g unsalted butter, melted
200g Greek yoghurt
2 teaspoons vanilla extract
2 large eggs

Syrup
450g caster sugar
450ml water
¼ teaspoon lemon juice
1 teaspoon rosewater

To decorate
100g blanched almonds
a few dried or fresh rose petals

If you are making a large cake, grease a 23cm x 33cm cake tin well. If using mini loaf cases, you don't need to grease them; just put them on a baking tray. You will need 15–20.

Place all the dry ingredients in a large bowl and stir to combine. Make a well in the centre and add the melted butter, yoghurt, vanilla and eggs. Mix with a wooden spoon or spatula until you have a smooth batter. Spoon it into the cake tin or loaf cases, tapping the loaf cases to level the mixture. Refrigerate for 1–2 hours.

Meanwhile, make the syrup. Combine the sugar, water and lemon juice in a small pan and bring to the boil. Boil for 2–3 minutes, then remove from the heat and stir in the rosewater.

Heat the oven to 180°C/Gas Mark 4. If making a large cake, score the top into diamond shapes with a knife and place a blanched almond in the centre of each one. The mini loaves don't need to be scored; simply decorate with the almonds. Bake until golden brown – about 40 minutes for a large cake, 20–25 minutes for the mini ones. Remove from the oven, pour the syrup on top, then bake for another 15 minutes. Take out of the oven and cut the large cake along the score lines. Leave to cool completely.

Serve decorated with dried or fresh rose petals.

35

Orange and Almond Cake
Spain

Some of the best oranges in the world come from the Valencia region of Spain. Almonds, too, are plentiful and can be found in Catalonia, Valencia, Murcia and Andalusia. It's no surprise, then, that oranges and almonds are often combined to make cakes and tarts. Olive oil would have been used as a substitute for butter and lends a very distinctive flavour and rich colour.

This cake seems to cook better when it is not more than 2.5cm deep, hence the fairly large tin size. It is quite soft and moist, and keeps well. Since you can prepare it the day before, it is very handy to serve as a dessert, with ice cream or cream

Makes a 25cm cake

4 large navel oranges
50ml light, fruity olive oil
5 eggs, separated
200g caster sugar
225g ground almonds, sifted

To prepare the cake tin
2 tablespoons olive oil
75g flaked almonds, chopped

To decorate
50g flaked almonds, toasted
a little icing sugar

Heat the oven to 170°C/Gas Mark 3. Grease a 25cm springform cake tin with the 2 tablespoons of olive oil and sprinkle the base and sides with the chopped flaked almonds.

Grate the zest from the oranges and set aside. Peel the oranges and chop them over a plate to catch any juice. Put the chopped oranges and their juice in a small saucepan and simmer gently until the oranges are soft and excess liquid has evaporated; they need to be quite dry. Leave to cool, then place in a blender with the olive oil and blend until smooth.

Place the egg whites in a large, grease-free bowl with half the caster sugar and whisk with an electric mixer until they form stiff peaks. In another bowl, whisk the egg yolks with the remaining sugar until pale and thick. Fold the puréed oranges and the orange zest into the egg yolk mixture using a large metal spoon, then gently fold in the ground almonds. Fold in a third of the egg whites, taking care not to lose any volume. Fold in the remaining egg whites.

Transfer the mixture to the prepared tin and sprinkle with any remaining flaked almonds. Bake for 20–25 minutes, until the cake is golden and a skewer inserted in the centre comes out clean. Leave the cake in the tin for 10 minutes before turning it out on to a wire rack to cool. Sprinkle with the toasted flaked almonds and dust with icing sugar. Serve warm or cold.

36 Raspberry Layer Cake
Canada

Raspberries and cream are the same colours as the famous Canadian flag, which is why this cake is made to celebrate Canada Day on 1st July. It is traditional to arrange the raspberries on top of the cake in a maple leaf shape, since this is depicted on the flag. Canada Day is a national holiday and there are many celebrations across the country, with fireworks, parades and, of course, cake. I include the pink cake pops for a modern take, but you can make it without them, if you prefer.

Makes a 20cm cake

Pink cake pops
75g very soft unsalted butter
75g caster sugar
1 medium egg
1 teaspoon milk
1 teaspoon vanilla extract
75g self-raising flour
a little pink food colouring

Vanilla cake
6 medium eggs
2 medium egg whites
150g caster sugar
½ teaspoon vanilla extract
150g plain flour, sifted

Raspberry syrup
100g caster sugar
100ml water
25g raspberries
1 tablespoon raspberry liqueur
   (optional)

Filling
1 litre double cream
25g icing sugar
1 teaspoon vanilla extract
3 tablespoons raspberry jam
300g raspberries

Heat the oven to 170°C/Gas Mark 3. Grease and flour 12 cake pop moulds.

Combine all the cake pop ingredients except the food colouring in a bowl and beat with an electric mixer for 2 minutes, until you have a smooth batter. Mix in the food colouring. Spoon or pipe the mixture into the cake pop moulds, filling them no more than half full. Bake for 15–18 minutes, until well risen and firm but not too brown. Leave to cool in the moulds.

To make the vanilla cake, grease three 20cm sandwich cake tins and line the bases with baking parchment. Grease again and flour the tins.

Place the eggs, egg whites and sugar in a large bowl and whisk with an electric mixer on high speed until pale and tripled in volume. Add the vanilla extract. Using a large metal spoon, fold in the sifted flour, taking care not to lose any volume.

Divide the mixture evenly between the 3 cake tins and drop the cake pops randomly into them. Level with a spatula and bake at 170°C/Gas Mark 3 for 20–25 minutes, until the top is golden brown and the cake springs back when pressed gently with your finger. Cool in the tin for 10 minutes before turning out on to a wire rack to cool completely.

Meanwhile, make the raspberry syrup. Put the sugar, water and raspberries into a pan and bring to the boil. Remove from the heat and allow to cool, then whisk so the raspberries break up. Add the raspberry liqueur, if using.

To make the filling, put the cream, icing sugar and vanilla into a bowl and whisk to medium peaks. Keep in the fridge until needed.

Turn over one of the layers of cake and remove the paper. Place on a cake card and, using a pastry brush, soak the cake with raspberry syrup. Spread the cake with half the raspberry jam, then spread or pipe a thick layer of cream on to the jam. Cover with about a quarter of the raspberries, add more cream and level the top. Layer the next sponge layer in the same way then top with the third sponge. Coat the outside of the cake with the remaining cream, using a palette knife or spatula. Decorate with the remaining raspberries and dust with a little icing sugar, if liked.

37

Sachertorte
Austria

This legendary chocolate cake traditionally has the word Sacher piped on top, but it has changed its appearance a lot in the last few years. It provides a fabulous base for pastry chefs to improvise their own versions. Daniel Pearce, my sous chef some years ago, once made a loaf-shaped Sachertorte, sliced it into ten very thin layers and sandwiched them together with a particularly delicious salted caramel. I loved it and decided to do my own take on the flavour combination. Here's my very modern version of the Sachertorte.

125g unsalted butter, at room
  temperature
125g caster sugar
6 medium eggs, separated
125g dark chocolate (70 per cent
  cocoa solids), melted
125g plain flour
a pinch of salt

Filling
150ml double cream
1 teaspoon sea salt
100g dulce de leche
300g good-quality milk chocolate,
  finely chopped

Glaze
3 gelatine leaves
60g cocoa powder
75ml water
125ml double cream
200g caster sugar

Heat the oven to 180°C/Gas Mark 4. Grease a 35cm x 28cm Swiss roll tin, line it with baking parchment, then grease again.

Cream the butter and three-quarters of the sugar together until light and fluffy. Beat in the egg yolks one at a time, then stir in the melted chocolate. Sift the flour and gently fold it in, using a large metal spoon. In a separate bowl, whisk the egg whites with the remaining sugar and the salt until they form stiff peaks. Fold the egg whites into the batter 2 tablespoons at a time, using the same metal spoon. Be careful not to over mix, as this will make the cake heavy.

Transfer the mixture to the prepared tin and bake for 18–20 minutes, until the cake has shrunk away from the sides of the tin and springs back when pressed lightly in the centre with your finger. Leave to cool in the tin for 15 minutes before turning it out paper-side down on to a wire rack to cool completely. Leave the cake overnight if at all possible; this will make it easier to handle when filling and decorating.

To make the filling, put the cream, salt and dulce de leche into a pan and bring to a rolling boil over a medium heat, stirring continuously. Pour the mixture over the chopped chocolate in a bowl, leave for 1 minute and then whisk lightly to make a smooth, shiny ganache. Cover the surface with cling film and leave at room temperature for at least 2–3 hours or overnight.

Peel the paper away from the cake and cut it along its length into 3 even strips. Put one piece on a sheet of baking parchment on a

board and spread evenly with a layer of ganache. Place another piece of sponge on top and spread with more ganache. Top with the third piece of sponge and then place in the fridge for an hour – this is important so the cake is firm enough to cut.

Meanwhile, make the glaze. Soak the gelatine in plenty of cold water for about 5 minutes, until completely soft. Squeeze out excess water and put the gelatine to one side in a small bowl. Sift the cocoa powder into a bowl and mix in the water to make a thick paste, whisking to keep it smooth. Put the cream and sugar in a pan and bring to the boil. Remove the pan from the heat and whisk in the cocoa powder paste. Add the soaked gelatine and whisk gently until it dissolves. Pass through a fine sieve into a bowl and cover the surface with cling film. Leave to cool until just warm.

Remove the cake from the fridge and place on a work surface, still on the paper. Using a long bread knife, cut the cake diagonally in half along its length. The easiest way to do this is to put the cake right on the edge of the work surface so that one of its long sides runs along the edge and, with the knife pointing upwards at a 45-degree angle, start cutting at one of the bottom corners nearest you and run it along to the diagonally opposite corner of the cake. The bottom of the knife blade should run along the edge of the table at all times. Now turn the cake halves back to back to make a triangle. Stick them together by spreading ganache on to one of the surfaces and pushing them together. Using a palette knife, coat the outside of the cake with the

remaining ganache to make a smooth surface. Chill for half an hour.

To glaze the cake, place it on a wire rack set over a tray. Check that the glaze is warm but not hot and is soft enough to flow over the cake. Using a large ladle, pour the glaze over the cake to cover it completely. Leave the cake on the wire rack for 15 minutes, then transfer it to a board. To serve, cut into slices with a sharp knife, cleaning the knife after each cut.

38

Pineapple Upside-down Cake
England

Upside-down cakes have featured in English cooking since the Middle Ages, when they were often known as tansy cakes. Tansy is a herb that was frequently added to apple or pear cakes. The cake would have been cooked in a skillet over an open fire and then inverted on to a plate.

The pineapple upside-down cake seems to have first occurred round about the time Jim Dole of the Hawaiian Pineapple Company started canning pineapples, in 1903. The combination of buttery caramel, tangy pineapple and those red cherries makes it as popular today as it was then. My recipe rather unconventionally contains marzipan, which gives it a gentle almond flavour and super-soft texture.

Makes a 20cm cake

125g yellow marzipan
190g unsalted butter, at room
    temperature
190g caster sugar
3 medium eggs
1 teaspoon vanilla extract
190g self-raising flour, sifted

For the pineapple topping
2 x 425g cans of pineapple rings in
    juice
75g unsalted butter
50g light soft brown sugar
a few glacé cherries

To finish
3 tablespoons smooth apricot jam
1 tablespoon water
50g flaked almonds, toasted and
    roughly chopped

Heat the oven to 170°C/Gas Mark 3. Drain the pineapple slices and place on kitchen paper to absorb the excess juice. Soften the 75g butter in a microwave or small pan so it is pliable but not melted. Brush it thickly over a 20cm dome mould or a 20cm round deep cake tin, being sure to use it all. Sprinkle the brown sugar evenly over it. Place one pineapple ring in the centre of the tin and arrange the others around it, cutting them in half where necessary to cover the sides of the tin. Place a cherry in the centre of each ring. Roughly chop the rest of the pineapple.

Break the marzipan into pieces and place in a freestanding electric mixer fitted with the paddle attachment. Add the butter and mix on a low speed until combined. Gradually add the sugar, keeping the mixture smooth and lump free. Increase the speed and beat until pale and fluffy. Lightly beat the eggs with the vanilla and add to the mixture a little at a time, beating well after each addition. Gently fold in the sifted flour with a large metal spoon.

Transfer a third of the mixture to the prepared cake tin and level the top. Cover it with half the chopped pineapple, then add another third of the cake mixture, smooth the surface and cover with the rest of the pineapple. Top with the remaining cake mixture and level the surface with a spatula.

Bake for 35–40 minutes, until the cake is golden brown and springs back when lightly pressed with your finger. Leave in the tin for 10 minutes, then invert on to a serving plate. Put the apricot jam in a small pan with the water and bring to the boil, whisking gently. Brush the hot jam over the cake, then press the toasted almonds around the base. It's great hot or cold. Serve with clotted cream for a luxurious treat.

39

Marble Cake
Denmark

Most probably invented in Germany, the marble cake has become a favourite Danish teatime treat. Denmark lies to the north of Germany and to this day there is still a small German community living in Jutland. It is not hard to see why the Danish love this cake so much: the ground almonds add moisture, while the orange gives it a beautiful aroma and flavour. Originally the dark marbling would have been produced by adding spices and molasses to flavour and colour the batter, but they have been replaced by cocoa powder and the cake is often flavoured with orange zest. This recipe is from Mr Bachmann, one of my mentors, and never fails to please.

Makes a 25cm cake

300g self-raising flour
2 teaspoons baking powder
335g unsalted butter, softened
335g caster sugar
115g ground almonds
6 large eggs
3 tablespoons milk
½ teaspoon vanilla extract
grated zest of 1 orange
grated zest of ½ lemon
2 tablespoons cocoa powder
3 tablespoons warm water

To decorate
2 large navel oranges
225g caster sugar
50ml water
250–500g dark chocolate (70 per cent cocoa solids), tempered (see pages 184–185) or 250–500g dark cocoa Candy Melts (see page 188), melted
300ml whipping cream

Heat the oven to 170°C/Gas Mark 3. Grease and flour a 25cm kugelhopf mould.

Sift the flour and baking powder together. Place the butter (which must be soft and squidgy) in a bowl and add the sugar, ground almonds, sifted flour mixture, eggs, milk, vanilla extract and citrus zests. Using an electric mixer, beat on high speed for 2–3 minutes, until pale and fluffy.

Mix the cocoa powder and warm water together until smooth. Transfer a third of the cake mixture to a separate bowl and, using a large metal spoon, combine with the cocoa powder mixture. Spoon the chocolate and the plain cake mixture randomly into the prepared tin. Take a small sharp, knife and draw it through them several times to create a marbled effect. Bake for 50–60 minutes, until the cake is golden brown and well risen; a skewer inserted in the centre should come out clean. Leave to cool in the tin for 20 minutes, then turn out on to a wire rack to cool completely.

Whilst the cake is cooking, make the orange decoration. Peel the zest from the oranges using a vegetable peeler, then trim off any white pith from the strips of zest. Cut the zest into fine strips. Place 75g of the sugar in a small pan with the water and bring to the boil. Add the strips of orange zest, turn down the heat and simmer for 8–10 minutes, until soft and tender. Remove from the heat and leave to cool in the syrup.

Remove all the white pith from the oranges with a sharp knife, then slice the oranges into thin rings. Place the remaining sugar in a heavy-based frying pan and allow to melt over a medium heat. As it starts to melt and colour, stir with a wooden spoon. Do not leave the pan unattended at any time, as the sugar will turn into caramel very quickly. Once the sugar has melted and is a light golden colour, add a tablespoon of water, taking care it does not splash out of the pan, as the caramel will be very hot. Add the orange slices and simmer gently for 3–4 minutes on each side, until they caramelise. Lift them out of the pan and put on to a plate to cool.

Place the cake on a wire rack with a tray under it. Using a large ladle and working as quickly as possible, pour the tempered chocolate or melted Candy Melts over the cake to cover it completely. Before the chocolate sets, lift the cake on to a clean plate or a cake card with a fish slice or scraper. You can reuse the chocolate on the tray by melting it again, passing it through a fine sieve to remove any cake crumbs and storing it in a clean container for another day. Alternatively, if you don't want to use as much as 500g chocolate, reduce it to 250g and just drizzle it over the cake.

Whip the cream to firm peaks and pipe it into the centre of the cake. Decorate with the caramelised orange slices and candied orange zest.

40

Bienenstich
Germany

The legend goes that a bee was attracted to the honey on this cake and the baker was stung whilst trying to swat it away – hence the name bienenstich, *or bee sting. If you like honey and nuts, then these little cakes are for you. The combination of honeyed almonds, soft, buttery dough and creamy vanilla custard is irresistible – well worth the effort of the several procedures needed to make the cakes. They are best eaten on the day of baking.*

Makes 16

75ml whole milk
240g strong white flour
7g easy-blend dried yeast
15g caster sugar
½ teaspoon salt
45g unsalted butter, melted
1 medium egg
1 teaspoon vanilla extract

Vanilla custard
1 medium egg
1 egg yolk
20g caster sugar
15g plain flour
5g cornflour
250ml double cream
250ml whole milk
1 teaspoon vanilla extract

Topping
60g unsalted butter
50g caster sugar
85g honey
a pinch of salt
65g flaked almonds

Warm the milk to blood heat in a small pan. Place all the other ingredients in an electric mixer fitted with a dough hook. Add the milk and mix on a low speed for about 2 minutes, until it forms a soft dough. Continue to let the dough work until it is soft and smooth and no longer sticks to the side of the bowl. This could take 15–20 minutes. Cover the bowl and leave in a warm place for 45–50 minutes, until doubled in size.

Meanwhile, make the vanilla custard. Put the egg, egg yolk, sugar, flour and cornflour in a bowl and mix to a smooth, lump-free paste. Add 50ml of the cream and mix well. Bring the milk and vanilla to the boil in a small saucepan. Pour the milk over the egg mixture, whisking until combined. Transfer the mix back to the pan and bring to the boil over a medium heat, whisking continuously. Reduce the heat and cook for 1–2 minutes, still whisking. Transfer to a clean bowl, cover the surface with cling film and leave to cool.

To make the topping, put the butter, sugar, honey and salt into a pan and bring to the boil, stirring constantly. Remove from the heat and stir in the almonds. The mixture will be very hot, so take care. Spoon it into 16 equal portions on a non-stick baking mat. Leave until cool enough to handle, then roll each portion into a ball.

Divide the dough into 16 pieces. Spin each piece of dough into a ball, then flatten into a circle 7–8cm in diameter. Place each one in a silicone mini-muffin mould and press down firmly again to flatten. Stab each one several times with a fork. Flatten the balls of topping and put them on top of the dough in the moulds. Cover with oiled cling film and and leave to rise for about 45 minutes, until doubled in size.

Heat the oven to 180°C/Gas Mark 4. Place the non-stick baking mat on a baking sheet and put the moulds on top; this will keep your baking tray free from the sticky topping if it bubbles over. Bake for 20–22 minutes, until the buns are cooked through and the top is bubbling and golden brown. Remove them from the oven and leave to cool in the moulds for 15 minutes, then turn out and transfer to a wire rack to cool completely.

While the cakes are cooling, whisk the remaining 200ml cream for the vanilla custard until it forms firm peaks. Whisk the cold vanilla custard so it becomes smooth and then fold in the whipped cream.

Cut the buns in half, pipe or spread the bottom portions with the vanilla custard, then replace the tops.

41

Bûche de Noël
France

This traditional log-shaped cake is made throughout France especially for Christmas. Many of the world's top pâtissiers are to be found in France, and such is the competition to outdo each other that they are always inventing new cakes or modernising traditional ones. The bûche de Noël has not escaped the makeover, and I adore the pretty designs, different flavours and stunning finishes. I hope you enjoy the traditional taste and modern finish of mine.

Meringue sticks

3 large egg whites
180g caster sugar

Cake

4 large eggs
125g caster sugar
25g cocoa powder
70g plain flour

Coffee syrup

50g caster sugar
50ml water
1 teaspoon ground espresso coffee

Ganache

100ml double cream
100g dark chocolate (70 per cent cocoa solids), finely chopped

Chestnut rum cream

190ml double cream
215g sweetened chestnut purée
15g icing sugar
15ml dark rum
3–4 marrons glacés, chopped

To decorate

a little icing sugar
a little cocoa powder
silver leaf (optional)

First make the meringue sticks. Heat the oven to 110°C/Gas Mark ¼. Line a baking sheet with baking parchment. Put the egg whites and a third of the sugar in a large, grease-free bowl. Using an electric mixer on medium speed, whisk them to medium peaks. Add another third of the sugar and continue to whisk until the mixture forms firm peaks. Add the remaining sugar and whisk for another 3–4 minutes, until the meringue is thick and glossy.

Put the meringue in a piping bag fitted with a 5mm plain nozzle. Pipe little dots the size of a 5p piece on the lined baking tray, spacing them about 5mm apart and pulling away as you pipe to create small peaks. Bake for an hour until crisp and dry. When they are ready, they should lift off the paper without sticking. Leave to cool on the tray.

Next make the cake. Heat the oven to 180°C/Gas Mark 4. Grease a Swiss roll tin, approximately 37cm x 28cm, line it with baking parchment and grease the paper.

Using an electric mixer, whisk the eggs with the sugar until they have trebled in volume and look pale and fluffy. Sift the cocoa powder and flour directly on top and fold them in with a large metal spoon. Transfer to the lined tin and bake for 10–15 minutes, until the sponge springs back when pressed lightly with your finger. Do not overcook the cake or it will be dry and crisp. Leave it to cool in the tin.

Place all the ingredients for the coffee syrup in a pan and bring to the boil. Remove from the heat and leave to steep for 10 minutes. Pass through a fine sieve and leave to cool

completely.

To make the ganache, bring the cream to the boil in a small saucepan. Pour it over the chocolate in a bowl and leave for 1 minute, then whisk gently to a smooth, shiny ganache. Leave until it reaches a soft, spoonable consistency.

Put all the ingredients for the chestnut rum cream except the marrons glacés in a bowl and whisk until stiff, then set aside.

Grease a 1-litre terrine mould and line it with cling film, letting it overhang the sides. Using the terrine mould as a guide, cut the sponge to fit it. You will need 5 pieces: one for the bottom, two for the sides, one to go in the centre of the terrine and one for the top (there's no need to cover the short sides). Line the mould with the bottom and side pieces, ensuring there are no gaps. Using a pastry brush, lightly soak the sponge with the coffee syrup.

Filling the mould with the ganache, sponge and chestnut rum cream can be uniform or random; both look good. Pipe in enough chestnut rum cream to cover the base, then randomly pipe or spoon in 5 or 6 dollops of ganache. Add a few pieces of marron glacé, pipe or spoon in a little more chestnut rum cream, so it comes about half way up the terrine, and level with a palette knife or spatula. Add the middle layer of the sponge and brush with coffee syrup, then repeat the filling process. Save a little filling to coat the outside so you can attach the meringues. Once the terrine is full, level the top with a spatula and cover with the remaining piece of sponge. Place in the fridge for

1–2 hours.

To turn the terrine out, pull gently on the cling film, invert the mould over a plate or cake card and tap the base. Peel off the cling film. Coat the outside with the leftover chestnut cream and attach the meringues to it. Dust with icing sugar and a little cocoa powder, then finish with pieces of silver leaf, if using.

42

Tourva
Cyprus

This soft coconut cake soaked with a fragrant cinnamon syrup is very popular in Cyprus. It is easy to make and keeps well in a tin for a few days. I was quite worried when I first made it, as the mixture was very firm. I didn't panic, stuck to the recipe and was rewarded with the most wonderful cake that has a lovely, crunchy top to complement its soft interior. Although it is traditionally served plain, I couldn't resist the temptation to jazz it up, and finished it with frosting and chunks of candied coconut. These delicious little cubes, produced by Whitworth, are a new ingredient for baking enthusiasts and can be found in the baking section of large supermarkets. Alternatively, you could use fresh coconut cut into cubes.

Makes a 20cm square cake or 8–10 individual ones

300ml vegetable oil
335g caster sugar
4 medium eggs
1 teaspoon vanilla extract
170g self-raising flour
1 teaspoon baking powder
225g desiccated coconut

Syrup
500g caster sugar
500ml water
1 cinnamon stick

Frosting
140g unsalted butter, at room
    temperature
280g icing sugar, sifted
1 teaspoon vanilla extract
1–2 tablespoons milk
To decorate
a few candied coconut chunks

Heat the oven to 170°C/Gas Mark 3. Grease and flour a 20cm square shallow cake tin or 8–10 individual square card cake cases.

Put the oil and sugar in a bowl and whisk with an electric mixer on high speed for 2 minutes. Add the eggs and vanilla, then continue to whisk on high speed for about 5 minutes, until light and fluffy. Sift the flour and baking powder into a bowl. Using a large metal spoon, fold them into the batter a little at a time, taking care not to over mix and lose volume. Finally, fold in the coconut. Put the mixture into the prepared cake tin or pipe or spoon it into the cake cases. Bake for 20–25 minutes, until the top is stable and golden brown and a skewer inserted in the centre comes out clean.

While the cake is in the oven, put all the ingredients for the syrup in a small pan and bring to the boil, stirring gently. Pass through a fine sieve.

If making a large cake, pour the warm syrup over it as soon as it comes out of the oven. If you have used the small card cases, brush on the syrup with a pastry brush. Leave the cakes to cool.

To make the frosting, put the softened butter in a bowl and beat in half the icing sugar with an electric mixer. Add the vanilla and the remaining icing sugar and beat again until pale and fluffy. Add the milk a little at a time, mixing on a low speed, until you have a spreadable frosting.

Frost the cakes with the icing and scatter over the coconut cubes. You can make the design in the photo by piling the frosting on top of each cake, then using a palette knife to smooth it off one side at a time, each time starting at a slightly different angle. If you have made a large cake, simply turn it out of the tin, cover it with the frosting and cut it into squares.

43 Chocolate Pomegranate Cake
Israel

Pomegranates are grown throughout Israel and are used in many different dishes. There can be as many as 600 seeds in one fruit. I adore this cake. Moist and divine, it has everything a good cake needs: brown sugar, treacle, spice, chocolate and, of course, pomegranates. Get cracking and try it – you won't be disappointed. The chocolate is in the icing rather than the cake itself, making for a great contrast of chocolate and spice. Serve with crème fraîche or Greek yoghurt as a dessert.

Makes a 23cm cake

330g plain flour
1 teaspoon ground ginger
½ teaspoon ground cardamom
1 teaspoon bicarbonate of soda
245ml buttermilk
2 medium eggs
270g dark soft brown sugar
1 tablespoon pomegranate molasses
  (or treacle)
150g treacle
100g unsalted butter, melted

Syrup
180ml pomegranate juice
170g caster sugar
6 cardamom pods, crushed
½ teaspoon rosewater

Chocolate glaze
20g unsalted butter, diced
120ml double cream
125g dark chocolate (70 per cent
  cocoa solids), finely chopped

To decorate
seeds from 1 large pomegranate

Heat the oven to 170°C/Gas Mark 3. Grease a 23cm springform cake tin or a petal cake tin and line the base with baking parchment.

Sift the flour, ginger, cardamom and bicarbonate of soda into a large mixing bowl. Make a deep well in the centre, add the buttermilk, eggs, sugar, molasses, treacle and melted butter and whisk until smooth. Pour into the prepared tin and bake for 45 minutes or until the cake is well risen and a skewer inserted in the centre comes out clean. Leave to cool in the tin.

To make the syrup, put the pomegranate juice, sugar and cardamom in a small pan and bring to the boil, stirring to dissolve the sugar. Boil for 2–3 minutes, then remove from the heat and add the rosewater. Pass through a fine sieve. Allow the syrup to cool slightly, then pour it over the cake in the tin. Leave in the tin for about 15 minutes before turning it out.

To make the glaze, put the butter and cream into a small pan and bring to the boil. Pour over the chocolate in a bowl and leave for 1 minute, then whisk gently to make a shiny glaze. Pour the glaze immediately over the cake and push it to the sides with a spatula, allowing it to fall over the edges slightly. Sprinkle with the pomegranate seeds.

44

Easter Dolls
Croatia

In Croatia, Easter would not be Easter without these babies, especially if you come from the Istria and Primorje regions. Leftover dough from Easter bread used to be shaped into dolls and given to children. The eggs would have been dyed red by tradition but I have it on good authority that any colour is acceptable. If you want to achieve a bold colour, use white eggs. They can be quite hard to get hold of but brown eggs will still look great and taste just the same.

Makes 15

300ml milk
500g strong white flour
1 teaspoon salt
7g easy-blend dried yeast
50ml runny honey
30ml vegetable oil
2 small eggs
grated zest of 1 lemon

Eggs
1 teaspoon salt
red food colouring (or whatever
   colour you prefer)
15 small white eggs

Egg wash
1 egg
1 egg yolk
a pinch of salt

To decorate (optional)
1–3 of the following:
50g granulated sugar
50g nibbed sugar
50g sesame seeds

Warm the milk to blood heat in a small pan. Sift the flour and salt into an electric mixer fitted with a dough hook and stir in the yeast. Add the milk, honey, oil, eggs and lemon zest and mix on a low speed to bring them together. Increase the speed to medium and mix until the dough is no longer sticky and starts to comes away from the side of the bowl, forming a ball; this can take up to 20 minutes. Cover the bowl with a damp cloth and leave to rise in a warm place for 1½ hours or until the dough has doubled in size.

Meanwhile, hard-boil the eggs. Bring a large pan of water to the boil and add the salt and a few drops of food colouring. Food colourings vary in strength, but add enough to give the water a vibrant colour; the eggs will be paler than the colour of the water. Reduce the heat to a simmer and carefully lower in the eggs. Turn up the heat so the water is at a gentle boil and cook for 7 minutes. Remove the eggs from the pan and leave to cool.

When the dough has risen, gently knock it back and divide it into 15 equal pieces. Divide each of these in two, making one piece slightly larger than the other. Cover and leave to rest for 5 minutes. Roll each piece into a sausage shape. Now make a T shape with the ropes of dough, laying the longer rope out to form the top part of the T and pressing one end of the shorter rope on to the centre of the longer rope.

Put an egg near the top of each T shape, just below the horizontal piece of dough, and press it into the dough slightly. Taking the two pieces at the top, bring them down around the sides of the egg like a scarf and begin braiding the 3 strips. Pinch them together at the end to seal.

Place the completed braids on a baking tray lined with baking parchment, cover with lightly oiled cling film and leave in a warm place until they rise slightly.

Heat the oven to 180°C/Gas Mark 4. Make the egg wash by whisking all the ingredients together, then passing them through a fine sieve. Using a pastry brush, apply the egg wash to the risen braids, being careful not to get it on the eggs. Then sprinkle with your choice of granulated sugar, sesame seeds and nibbed sugar, or leave plain. Bake for 25–30 minutes, until golden brown. Check the bases are brown too before removing from the oven. Allow to cool, then paint on the dolls' faces with a felt-tip pen.

45 Helsinki Caramel Cakes
Finland

Karl Fazer Café in Helsinki is the place to go for cake. Established in 1891, it has a devoted following. The cakes are gloriously displayed in cabinets and on stands, tempting all those who pass by. Its version of this caramel cake is a must if you are visiting Helsinki.

This is a light sponge topped with a fudgy caramel icing. I make mine in small bun tins as they are so sweet, and sandwich them together with a little vanilla-flavoured cream to add some moisture and cut the sweetness. Making the icing is a slightly tricky procedure involving hot caramel. Please take extra cake to avoid burning yourself. The sugar gets very hot and needs quite a bit of stirring to crystallise it.

Makes 16

165g self-raising flour
½ teaspoon salt
215g unsalted butter, at room temperature
170g caster sugar
2 medium eggs
1 teaspoon vanilla extract
125ml milk

Filling
300ml double cream
1 teaspoon vanilla extract
25g icing sugar

Caramel icing
85g unsalted butter
440ml evaporated milk
390g caster sugar
1 teaspoon vanilla extract
½ teaspoon bicarbonate of soda

To decorate
50g flaked almonds, toasted
50g hazelnuts, toasted and roughly chopped
10g sea salt

Heat the oven to 170°C/Gas Mark 3. Grease and flour 16 holes of two 12-hole bun tins.

Sift the flour and salt together. Put the butter and sugar in a bowl and cream with an electric mixer on medium-high speed for about 5 minutes, until pale and fluffy. Lightly beat the eggs with the vanilla, then add to the mixture a little at a time, beating well after each addition. Using a large metal spoon, fold in a third of the flour, followed by a third of the milk; repeat until all the ingredients are incorporated.

Pipe or spoon the batter into the prepared bun tins, filling them about half full. Bake for 18–20 minutes, until the cakes are golden brown and spring back when pressed lightly with your finger. Let them cool in the tins for 5 minutes, then invert on to wire racks and leave to cool completely.

Put all the ingredients for the filling into a bowl and whisk until they form medium peaks. Transfer to a piping bag fitted with a plain 1cm nozzle, pipe a layer over the base of 8 of the cakes and sandwich together with the other 8. Put the cakes on a wire rack ready for covering with the caramel icing.

Put the butter and evaporated milk in a small pan and warm gently over a medium heat. Remove from the heat and cover to keep warm. Place a third of the sugar in a large, heavy-based pan and stir over a medium to high heat with a wooden spoon until it starts to melt and caramelise. It should be a golden brown colour. Repeat twice with the remaining sugar. Slowly pour the warm milk mixture on to the caramel, taking care as the caramel will spit and bubble. Bring back to the boil, stirring gently. Attach a sugar thermometer to the side of the pan and cook, stirring constantly with a wooden spoon, until the thermometer reads 111°C. Remove from the heat and immediately stir in the vanilla and bicarbonate of soda; the mixture will bubble up. Once it has settled, use a handheld electric mixer on a low-medium speed to beat it until it has a coating consistency; this will take about a minute.

Working quickly, pour the caramel sauce over the cakes. Sprinkle them with the almonds, hazelnuts and sea salt. Let the caramel set before handling them.

46

Honey Cake
Croatia

This is one of the most popular desserts in Croatia and consists of honey sponge soaked with rum syrup and layered with honey and chocolate custard. I really like the way it looks when cut into oblongs.

400g plain flour
1 tablespoon bicarbonate of soda
45ml whole milk
45ml vegetable oil
30g light runny honey
150g caster sugar
1 medium egg, lightly beaten
a little icing sugar

Honey and chocolate custard
1 vanilla pod
500ml whole milk
75g runny honey
75g caster sugar
6 tablespoons fine semolina
200g unsalted butter, diced
100g dark chocolate (70 per cent cocoa solids), chopped

Rum syrup
100g caster sugar
100ml water
50ml dark rum

Sift together the flour and bicarbonate of soda, then repeat twice. Put the milk, oil, honey and sugar in a pan and place over a low heat until the honey and sugar dissolve, stirring continuously. Remove from the heat and leave to cool until hand hot. Add the flour and egg, mix by hand until everything starts coming together, then knead gently into a soft dough. Wrap the dough in cling film and leave to rest in the fridge for 15 minutes.

Take 2 Swiss roll tins, approximately 37cm x 28cm, and cut a piece of baking parchment to fit the base of each one. Cut the dough in half. Roll out one piece of dough on one piece of baking parchment, then carefully lift it, still on the paper, into a Swiss roll tin. Repeat with the second piece of dough.

Heat the oven to 180°C/Gas Mark 4. Bake both tins of dough in the centre of the oven for 5 minutes, until barely set. It should feel firm to the touch but still be pale. Take care not to over bake, or it will become fragile and crisp. Remove from the oven and immediately cut each sheet neatly in half across its width. Leave to cool in the trays.

Meanwhile, make the custard. Slit the vanilla pod open lengthwise and put it in a small pan with the milk, honey and sugar. Bring to the boil and then remove from the heat. Whisk in the semolina and return to a low heat, whisking constantly until it thickens. Remove from the heat and take out the vanilla pod. Scrape the seeds from the pod into the mixture and whisk to combine.

Transfer to a mixing bowl, cover the surface with cling film and leave to cool until it is hand hot. Whisk in the butter a little at a time, mixing well after each addition. Transfer to a clean bowl, cover the surface with cling film and leave to cool. Melt the chocolate in a microwave or in bowl set over a pan of gently simmering water, making sure the water doesn't touch the base of the bowl. Transfer a third of the filling to a separate bowl and stir in the chocolate. Keep both fillings covered.

To make the syrup, bring the sugar and water to the boil in a small pan, stirring to dissolve the sugar. Remove from the heat and add the rum.

To assemble the cake, place one piece on a square cake card and, using a pastry brush, soak it with about a quarter of the warm rum syrup. Spread half the honey custard evenly over the cake. Place another sponge layer on top and press down gently. Soak it with rum syrup, then spread the chocolate custard on top. Add a third layer of cake, press down gently and soak with more rum syrup. Spread the remaining honey custard over it, cover with the last layer of sponge and soak with the remaining syrup. (If you did over bake the base, put the cake in an airtight container and leave in the fridge overnight; it will soften considerably.) Trim the sides with a sharp knife, then cut the cake into 8 rectangles. Dust with a little icing sugar before serving.

47

Kransekake
Norway

The original version of this cake was shaped like an overflodighetshorn, *or horn of plenty, made up of many rings and filled with sweets and cookies. Perhaps it was easier to build it upright and so it gradually became a tower of rings. Either way, it is pretty advanced and not for the fainthearted. The rings are quite crumbly and take a lot of patience to form. Mine broke up a little but I did find that if you put the pieces into the cake tins, they join together during baking – a joy to discover, as there are so many rings.*

You will need to buy a set of nonstick kransekake rings. They can often be found on Amazon or eBay.

225g unsalted butter, at room
   temperature
250g marzipan
220g icing sugar, sifted
2 teaspoons almond extract
4 egg yolks
500g plain flour, sifted

Royal icing
2 medium egg whites
450g icing sugar, sifted
1 teaspoon lemon juice

Heat the oven to 170°C/Gas Mark 3. Put the butter and marzipan into a freestanding electric mixer fitted with the paddle attachment and cream on a low speed until they form a smooth paste. Gradually add the icing sugar, followed by the almond extract and egg yolks, mixing on a low speed to combine. With the machine on very low, slowly add the flour to form a soft but not sticky dough. Do not over mix or make it too aerated.

Transfer the dough to a lightly floured work surface and knead lightly until smooth. Roll it into long, thin snake shapes that will fit inside the cake rings. Gently pick up a piece of dough, supporting it with your hands, and place it in one of the rings, then pinch the ends together – start with the smaller rings first, as they are easier. If the dough breaks, don't worry; just lay the pieces in the rings, as they will join together during baking. As soon as you have enough rings to fill the oven, start to bake them in batches, cooking similar sizes together. Bake in the centre of the oven for 15–18 minutes, until very lightly browned. Leave in the rings to cool.

To make the royal icing, put the egg whites in a freestanding electric mixer fitted with the whisk attachment and add a couple of tablespoons of the icing sugar. Whisk for 1–2 minutes on a high speed. Keep adding the icing sugar, 2–3 tablespoons at a time, whisking well for 1–2 minutes after each addition. When the icing is thick and white, add the lemon juice to achieve a softer piping consistency; it should hold its shape but be soft enough to pipe easily. Transfer to a disposable piping bag and cut a small hole in the tip.

To assemble the cakes, I recommend stacking them up first without the icing to make sure they are even and in the right order. It does get a little confusing otherwise. You will need a 30cm round, thick cake card or a flat plate. Pipe a little icing on the base of the largest ring and flip it over icing-side down on to the cake card or plate. This will prevent it slipping off later. Pipe some icing in scallops around the edge of the ring on the cake card, then pipe a circle of icing nearer the centre. Put the next cake ring on top – the circle of icing will hold it in place. Pipe icing on the second cake ring in the same way and put it on top of the first. Continue to do this until all the layers have been decorated and fixed in place. Dust with a little icing sugar. The cake will keep for 3–4 days and can be broken into pieces for eating.

48

Rainbow Rice Cake
Korea

This is a good example of how dramatically cakes can differ throughout the world. It's not very sweet and has an unusual texture for a cake as European standards go. I nervously offered a Korean friend a piece and she assured me that I had made it correctly. It is so pretty that I like to cover the whole thing in sprinkles – not very Korean, I am sure, but I love the look.

You need to buy frozen glutinous rice flour, available from Korean shops. Avoid the sweetened option, as I have added sugar to the recipe. Don't be tempted to substitute other types of rice flour, as the cake will not hold together and you will end up with a lot of coloured flour that falls apart even after much steaming – as I found out more than once.

Makes an 18cm square cake

White layer
200g rice flour
a pinch of salt
30g caster sugar
2 tablespoons cold water

Purple layer
200g rice flour
a pinch of salt
30g caster sugar
2 tablespoons cold water
a few drops of purple food colouring

Green layer
200g rice flour
a pinch of salt
30g caster sugar
2 tablespoons cold water
1 teaspoon mugwort tea or green tea powder
a drop of green food colouring

Yellow layer
200g rice flour
30g caster sugar
a pinch of salt
1 tablespoon lemon juice
1 tablespoon cold water
a few drops of yellow food colouring

Pink layer
200g rice flour
a pinch of salt
30g caster sugar
2 tablespoons cold water
a few drops of pink food colouring

To decorate
60ml double cream, whipped
  (or a little buttercream)
2–3 tubs of coloured hundreds and
  thousands

Place 500ml water in a steamer that is large enough to hold the tin. Grease an 18cm square deep cake tin and line the base and sides with baking parchment.

The method for each layer is the same. I suggest weighing the ingredients for all the layers before you start making them, as this takes the most time.

Place the rice flour and salt into a large, wide bowl, add the sugar and whisk to combine. Add the water, food colouring and the flavouring, if there is any. Rub the ingredients through your fingertips to get rid of any lumps. Keep mixing until it has a texture like breadcrumbs. Transfer the mixture to a large sieve and sift it into a clean bowl. Tip the sifted mix into the cake tin and flatten it out so it is level. I used a plastic bowl scraper for this. Repeat the process for the other layers, adding them to the tin as you go.

Bring the water in the steamer to a simmer, place the tin in the steamer and cover with a lid. Steam for 30 minutes, until the cake feels firm to the touch. Leave for another 5–10 minutes, if necessary.

Remove the cake from the steamer and leave to cool in the tin. Turn it out and cover the outside with a very thin layer of whipped cream, then cover completely with the hundreds and thousands. Best eaten on the day it is made.

49

Lemon Genoese Cakes
Italy

I always thought the Genoese cake came from France but, although it is associated with many French cakes, it originated from Genoa – hence the name. It was one of the first cakes I ever learned to make. Light and fluffy, it relies on whisking the eggs with the sugar to create volume, rather than the addition of a raising agent. It doesn't keep well and benefits from being soaked in a flavoured syrup, as it can become dry very quickly. Having said that, it is great eaten on the day it is made.

I have broken away from tradition here and baked my Genoese cake in these adorable little flowerpot moulds, available from Lakeland. Muffin tins would work just as well.

Makes 12

125g caster sugar
4 large eggs
125g plain flour
25g unsalted butter, melted
grated zest of 1 lemon

Lemon curd
2 large eggs
75g caster sugar
75g unsalted butter, diced
juice and grated zest of 2 lemons

Lemon syrup
60g caster sugar
juice of 2 lemons

To decorate
a little icing sugar
250g green ready-to-roll icing
2 Oreo cookies, with the filling removed
an assortment of ready-made icing flowers and insects (see page 188)

Heat the oven to 170°C/Gas Mark 3. Grease and flour 12 silicone flowerpot moulds.

Place the sugar and eggs in a large bowl and whisk with an electric mixer for 5–8 minutes, until thick, pale and tripled in volume. Sift the flour on to a sheet of baking parchment. Using a large metal spoon, fold it into the mixture a third at a time, taking care not to over mix and lose volume. Pour the melted butter around the edge and fold it in. Finally, fold in the grated lemon zest. Pipe or spoon the mixture into the prepared moulds.

Bake for 18–20 minutes, until the cakes are risen and springy to the touch. Remove from the oven and set aside until cool enough to handle. Turn out on to a wire rack to cool completely.

Meanwhile, make the lemon curd. Place all the ingredients in a bowl set over a pan of simmering water, making sure the water doesn't touch the base of the bowl. Whisk gently with a hand whisk until the curd thickens enough to leave a trail on the surface; this can take 10–15 minutes. If you have a blender, pour the hot curd into it as soon as it thickens and blitz on high for 1–2 minutes to lighten it. Pour into a bowl, cover the surface with cling film and leave to cool.

To make the syrup, put the sugar and lemon juice in a small pan and bring to the boil, stirring to dissolve the sugar. Allow to cool slightly before using.

Remove the middle of each cake with a cupcake corer, an apple corer or a small, sharp knife; keep the pieces you remove. Using a pastry brush, soak the inside of the cakes with the lemon syrup. Pipe or spoon in the lemon curd. Cut the tops off the cake pieces you removed and use them as a cover for the curd, making the tops of the cakes level again. Spread a little of the remaining lemon curd on top of the cakes to secure the icing.

Lightly dust a work surface with icing sugar and roll out the icing to about 1cm thick. Using a pastry cutter, cut out discs the same size as the tops of the flowerpots and lay them on top of the cakes, pressing down gently to secure in place.

Take small balls of the remaining green icing and push them through a tea strainer to make it look like moss. Remove the moss from the tea strainer with a small knife and place it on top of the cakes in small clumps.

To make the soil, put the Oreo cookies in a small plastic food bag and crush them with a rolling pin. Spoon on top of the cakes and decorate with the edible flowers and insects.

50

Pistachio Cakes
Iran

Often eaten at weddings and funerals, pistachio nuts are an integral part of Iranian culture. They have long been mentioned in literature and are an essential part of many beliefs and traditions. No celebrations can take place without them.

I recommend you serve these adorable cakes as a dessert with yoghurt and a little honey or fruit compote such as plum. I turned mine out of the moulds and popped them into colourful little card cups.

Makes 12

225g pistachio nuts
150g unsalted butter, at room
    temperature
120g caster sugar
2 medium eggs, lightly beaten
20g plain flour
20g cornflour

To decorate
2 tablespoons apricot jam
1 tablespoon water
100g pistachio nuts

Heat the oven to 170°C/Gas Mark 3. Finely chop 75g of the pistachio nuts and finely grind the rest. Grease a 12-cup muffin tin or silicone mould and sprinkle with the chopped nuts.

Using an electric mixer, cream the butter and sugar together until pale and fluffy. Add the eggs a little at a time, beating well after each addition. Fold in the ground pistachio nuts with a large metal spoon. Sift the flour and cornflour together and fold them into the mixture. Spoon or pipe it into the prepared moulds.

Bake the cakes for 20–25 minutes, until they are lightly coloured and spring back when pressed gently with your finger. Cool in the moulds for 15 minutes, then turn out on to a wire rack to cool completely.

Gently heat the jam with the water until runny, then strain through a sieve. Brush it on to the cakes and sprinkle with the pistachios.

51

Irish Coffee Cake
Ireland

On a cold, wet night in 1942, Joe Sheridan, a chef in Foynes, County Limerick, welcomed a group of tired Americans from a Pan Am flying boat with hot coffee sweetened with sugar, boosted with Irish whiskey and topped with double cream. When one of the passengers asked if the coffee was Brazilian, Joe replied that it was Irish, and thus 'Irish coffee' was born.

It wasn't until the 1960s that recipes for Irish coffee cake started to appear in cookbooks. This one contains the essential components of intensely flavoured coffee syrup, an indecent amount of Irish whiskey and lashings of thick cream. It is best eaten on the day it is made.

Makes an 18cm cake

180g unsalted butter, at room temperature
180g caster sugar
3 large eggs
1 teaspoon vanilla extract
180g self-raising flour
a pinch of salt
5 teaspoons strong instant coffee, dissolved in 3 tablespoons hot water

Coffee syrup
150ml strong black coffee
120g caster sugar
3 tablespoons Irish whiskey

Filling
300ml double cream
a few drops of vanilla extract
60g icing sugar
2 tablespoons Irish whiskey

Coating
200ml whipping cream
a few drops of vanilla extract
25g icing sugar
2 tablespoons Irish whiskey

To decorate
100ml water
1 teaspoon instant coffee
1 teaspoon agar agar flakes

Chocolate shavings
300g dark chocolate (70 per cent cocoa solids), tempered (see pages 184–185)

Heat the oven to 170°C/Gas Mark 3. Grease and flour an 18cm square deep cake tin.

Using an electric mixer, cream the butter and sugar together until pale and fluffy. Lightly beat the eggs with the vanilla and add them to the mixture a little at a time, beating well after each addition. Sift the flour and salt together. Fold two-thirds of the flour into the cake mixture with a large metal spoon, then add the dissolved coffee and mix just to combine. Fold in the remaining flour.

Transfer the mixture to the prepared cake tin and level the top. Bake for 35–40 minutes, until the top springs back when pressed lightly with your finger and a skewer inserted in the centre comes out clean. Leave in the tin for 10 minutes, then turn out on to a wire rack to cool.

To make the coffee syrup, bring the coffee and sugar to the boil in a pan, stirring to dissolve the sugar. Remove from the heat and add the whiskey. Leave to cool.

Whisk all the ingredients for the filling together until they form firm peaks; take care not to over whisk.

Cut the cake horizontally into 3 layers. Place the bottom layer on a cake card and soak it well with the syrup, using a pastry brush. Spread with some of the filling in an even layer about 5mm thick, then put the middle piece of sponge on top and soak with more syrup. Spread it with the remainder of the filling. Top with the remaining layer of cake and soak well. Press down gently to level the cake.

Whisk all the ingredients for the coating together until they form medium peaks. Coat the outside of the cake completely with the mixture, making sure the top is level.

For the decoration, bring the water to the boil in a pan, add the coffee and stir to dissolve. Remove from the heat, add the agar agar flakes and stir until dissolved, then leave to cool. Agar agar sets quickly, so keep an eye on the mix until it is cold but not set. Working quickly, drizzle and flick the coffee mixture over the cake with a teaspoon to give an abstract design. Put the cake into the fridge whilst you prepare the chocolate for the outside.

To make the chocolate shavings, pour the chocolate on to a very cold marble surface and quickly spread with a palette knife to level it out as thinly as possible. As soon as the chocolate has set, take a large chopping knife and, holding it at a flat angle, shave the chocolate off the marble in roughly 5cm pieces. It really does not matter if they are all sorts of shapes and sizes. If the chocolate breaks, it is because it has

become too cold. You can scrape it off, melt it and try again. If all this seems too much, just grate the chocolate with a cheese grater.

Remove the cake from the fridge and push the chocolate shavings into the cream on the sides of the cake, slightly overlapping them.

52

Lemon and Thyme Drizzle Cakes
England

The lemon drizzle cake is firmly established in the English cake repertoire but I don't quite know how it came about. It's a variation on a classic sponge cake, and modern versions tend to be made by the all-in-one method. I like to speculate that the lemon drizzle part was due to Mr Kipling's fondness for drizzling his fondant fancies and other cakes with icing. One thing is for sure: it has become a national favourite at teatime.

I have flavoured this version with a little thyme, which complements the lemon. You can use any type of edible flower, including flowering herbs. If you are not sure whether your flowers are edible, always check first by looking them up online or in a gardening book. Better safe than sorry.

I use little silicone dome moulds to make these cakes. They are available from Lakeland, which sells them under the name of chocolate teacake moulds.

Makes 12

225g unsalted butter, at room temperature
225g self-raising flour
225g caster sugar
3 large eggs
grated zest of 2 lemons
2 teaspoons chopped thyme

To decorate

1 egg white
5 sprigs of thyme
100g caster sugar
10–20 edible flowers, such as violas, pansies and violets, washed and patted dry

Lemon syrup

juice of 2 lemons
50g icing sugar

Filling

250ml whipping cream
½ teaspoon vanilla extract
20g icing sugar

Lemon icing

1 egg white
150–200g icing sugar
juice of 2 lemons

Start by making the crystallised thyme for the decoration. Brush the egg white on to the thyme with a small paintbrush. Put the caster sugar into a bowl and drop in the thyme sprigs, then toss them gently with a spoon to coat them in the sugar. Lift them out of the sugar and lay them on a tray lined with baking parchment. Leave to dry for a couple of hours in a warm place, such as an airing cupboard or near a heater.

Heat the oven to 180°C/Gas Mark 4. Grease and flour two 6-indentation small dome silicone moulds.

Now make the cakes. Make sure the butter is soft and pliable for the best results. Warm it a little in a microwave or in a bowl set over a pan of simmering water and mush to a pliable texture by hand, if necessary. Sift the flour twice. Place all the cake ingredients in a food processor or a freestanding electric mixer and blend for 1–2 minutes, until the mixture is just combined, thick and smooth. Spoon or pipe the cake batter into the prepared moulds, filling them half way – you should have half the cake mixture left, as you will have to make

2 batches. Bake for about 25 minutes, until well risen and pale golden brown. Remove from the oven and cool in the moulds for 5 minutes, then turn them out on to a wire rack to cool completely. Clean the moulds, grease and flour them, then fill and bake as before. You will have 12 cakes in total once sandwiched.

Wash and dry the moulds. Stab the surface of the cakes several times with a cocktail stick or skewer. Now place the lemon juice and icing sugar for the lemon syrup in a small pan, bring to the boil and simmer for 1–2 minutes. Pop half the cakes back into the moulds and spoon over the hot syrup. Carefully turn them out of the moulds on to a wire rack, then repeat with the remaining cakes .

Whisk the cream with the vanilla and icing sugar until it forms firm peaks. Use the cream to sandwich the cakes together to make a ball.

To make the icing, put the egg white in a bowl, sift in about 75g of the icing sugar and whisk with an electric mixer for about 3 minutes, until smooth. Gradually whisk in another 75g icing sugar and continue whisking until the mixture is thick enough to leave a trail on the surface, adding more icing sugar if necessary. Mix in the lemon juice a little at a time until the icing becomes thin enough to drizzle over the cakes.

Drizzle the icing over the cakes from a teaspoon or a small piping bag with a hole snipped in the tip, letting it run down the sides of the cakes. Decorate them with the crystallised thyme and the flowers. Leave the cakes for 20 minutes for the icing to set before serving.

53

Streuselkuchen
Germany

This cake is enjoyed in a variety of guises all around the world, but always includes a crumble topping. Traditionally it would have been a yeasted cake, made in a shallow tray so that it was no more than about 2.5cm thick. In modern versions the yeast cake has become more biscuit like and may include seasonal fruit. Soft cheese is added to many German cakes, and gives this particular recipe an extra depth of flavour. I have used raspberries here but it also works well with plums.

Makes a 25cm cake

225g plain flour
1 teaspoon ground mixed spice
1 teaspoon ground ginger
1 teaspoon ground cinnamon
75g caster sugar
150g unsalted butter, at room
   temperature
1 teaspoon vanilla extract

Cream cheese filling
125g cream cheese
115g caster sugar
1 teaspoon vanilla extract
1 egg yolk

Raspberry filling
250g good-quality raspberry jam
a few drops of lemon juice
100g raspberries

Streusel topping
100g light soft brown sugar
100g ground almonds
100g unsalted butter, diced
60g plain flour
1 tablespoon ground cinnamon
100g pecan nuts, chopped

Heat the oven to 170°C/Gas Mark 3. Grease a 25cm square shallow cake tin and line the base with baking parchment.

Sift the flour and spices into the bowl of a freestanding electric mixer. Add the sugar, butter and vanilla and, using the paddle attachment, mix on a low speed until everything comes together to form a firm dough. Press into the base of the tin in an even layer. Bake for about 20 minutes, until light brown, then remove from the oven and leave to cool.

To make the cream cheese filling, put the cheese, sugar and vanilla in a bowl and beat with a wooden spoon to combine. Add the egg yolk and mix well. Spread the filling over the cake in the tin. Combine all the ingredients for the raspberry filling and spoon on top of the cheese filling.

For the streusel topping, put all the ingredients except the nuts in a bowl and rub them together with your fingertips until they resemble chunky pieces of crumble. Stir in the nuts, then sprinkle the streusel over the cake. Return to the oven and bake for 40–45 minutes, until the topping is lightly browned. Leave to cool in the tin. Cut into oblongs or squares to serve.

54

Rocky Road Cheesecake
USA

These adorable little baked chocolate cheesecakes feature an Oreo cookie base, which adds a slightly salty taste. It's a great combination and includes all the elements of the famous Rocky Road: marshmallows, nuts, chocolate and cherries. I use griottine cherries, which pack an alcoholic punch; you might prefer to substitute glacé cherries if you are making this for children.

Makes 12

100g dark chocolate (70 per cent
　cocoa solids)
50g white chocolate
500g full-fat cream cheese
1 teaspoon vanilla extract
125g caster sugar
3 medium eggs

Base
14 Oreo cookies, crushed
45g unsalted butter, melted

To decorate
100g dark chocolate (70 per cent
　cocoa solids), melted
100g salted roasted peanuts
1 bag of mini marshmallows
1 bag of mini Oreo cookies
12 griottine cherries

First make the base. Heat the oven to 170°C/Gas Mark 3. Put the Oreo cookies in a plastic bag and crush to fine crumbs with a rolling pin. Transfer them to a mixing bowl and stir in the melted butter. Take a 12-cup muffin tin and spoon a tablespoon of the crumbs into each hole, pressing them down to level. Bake for 10 minutes, then remove from the oven and set aside. Reduce the oven temperature to 140°C/Gas Mark 1.

To make the cheesecake, melt the dark and white chocolate together in a microwave or in a bowl set over a pan of gently simmering water, making sure the water doesn't touch the base of the bowl. Using an electric mixer on a low speed, mix together the cream cheese, vanilla extract and sugar until smooth. Do not over mix. Add the eggs and mix until combined. With the mixer still on a low speed, gradually mix in the melted chocolate.

Pour the mixture into the muffin tins and bake for 40–45 minutes, until the top is firm and they are no longer wobbly. Be careful not to let them soufflé up or they will be overdone. Remove from the oven and leave to cool in the tins. I find it easiest to put them in the freezer for an hour before turning out of the tins, then they pop right out.

To finish, pour some of the melted chocolate on top of each cheesecake, then sprinkle with the peanuts, marshmallows, mini Oreo cookies and griottine cherries. Drizzle with more melted chocolate.

55

Polish Easter Cake
Poland

This yeasted cake is known as babka *in Poland, meaning 'grandmother' – possibly because of the shape, which is said to resemble an old woman's wide, swirling skirt. It is a favourite at Easter time, when butter and eggs return to the diet after Lent. Traditionally soaked with rum, it can be iced with a lemon glaze or left plain.*

Makes a 25cm cake

250ml milk
500g plain flour
1 teaspoon salt
7g easy-blend dried yeast
170g caster sugar
170g unsalted butter
3 medium eggs
grated zest of 2 lemons
1 teaspoon vanilla extract
170g raisins

Rum syrup
200g caster sugar
150ml water
50ml dark rum

Lemon curd glaze
2 medium eggs
65g unsalted butter, diced
65g caster sugar
juice and grated zest of 2 large
    lemons

To decorate (optional)
1 bag of chocolate mini eggs
a few sugarpaste flowers

Grease and flour a 25cm kugelhopf or bundt tin. Warm the milk to blood heat in a small pan. Place the flour, salt, yeast and sugar into a freestanding electric mixer fitted with the dough hook. Melt the butter and let it cool slightly. Add the milk, eggs, grated lemon zest, vanilla extract and raisins to the flour, together with the melted butter, and mix on a low speed for 1–2 minutes to form a soft, slightly sticky dough. Scrape the mixture into the prepared tin, cover with lightly oiled cling film and leave in a warm place for up to an hour, until doubled in size.

Heat the oven to 180°C/Gas Mark 4. Bake the cake for 45–50 minutes until golden brown. Remove from the oven, let the cake cool in the tin, then turn it out. Wash and dry the tin.

To make the rum syrup, bring the sugar and water to the boil, stirring to dissolve the sugar, then remove from the heat and stir in the rum. Put the cake back in the tin and pour over the hot syrup. Leave for a few minutes so the cake soaks up the syrup, then invert it on to a plate or serving dish.

Place all the ingredients for the lemon curd glaze in a bowl set over a pan of gently simmering water, making sure the water doesn't touch the base of the bowl. Mix until the butter melts and all the ingredients are combined. Whisk gently over the pan of water for about 15 minutes, until the curd thickens enough to leave a trail on the surface. Pass through a fine sieve into a bowl or measuring jug.

Pour the warm curd over the cake to glaze. Don't worry about the excess glaze if it drips on to the plate. It does not have to coat the cake evenly.

When the glaze is set to the touch, decorate with the mini eggs and sugarpaste flowers, if using.

56

Red Velvet Cake
USA

When red velvet cake was invented, the vibrant colour came from the acidity of the vinegar reacting with the buttermilk and the anthocyanins in the cocoa powder. Today's cocoa powders are alkalised, which means you need to add some red food colouring to achieve a really strong shade of red. It's said that the Adams Extract Company invented a version of this cake using its liquid red colouring to help boost falling sales during the Great Depression. Regardless of who came up with the modern recipe, it is currently enjoying a revival and I urge you to give it a go. It's really simple to make and the mixture can be used for cupcakes too.

Makes a 17cm cake

220g plain flour
260g caster sugar, plus a little extra for dusting
1 teaspoon baking powder
1 teaspoon bicarbonate of soda
1 teaspoon cocoa powder
1 medium egg
40ml buttermilk
130ml vegetable oil
40g good-quality ready-made custard
1 tablespoon liquid red food colouring

Cream cheese frosting
300g cream cheese
75g icing sugar
75ml double cream, whipped
½ teaspoon vanilla extract

Heat the oven to 170°C/Gas Mark 3. Grease a 35cm x 25cm Swiss roll tin and line the base with baking parchment. Grease the paper again.

Sift the flour, sugar, baking powder, bicarbonate of soda and cocoa powder into a large bowl, then repeat. In a separate bowl, mix the egg, buttermilk, oil, custard and red colouring together. Make a well in the centre of the dry ingredients and pour in the wet ingredients. Use a hand whisk to combine them to a smooth batter. Pour into the prepared tin and level with a spatula. Bake for 20–25 minutes, until the cake springs back when pressed gently with your finger and a skewer inserted in the centre comes out clean. Leave to cool in the tin for 10 minutes, then turn out on to a sheet of baking parchment dusted with a little caster sugar.

To make the frosting, beat the cream cheese and icing sugar together for 1 minute, using an electric mixer. Add the cream and vanilla and beat for another minute, until smooth and creamy.

To assemble the cake, you will need a 17cm heart template or a 17.5cm round template. Using the template and a small, sharp knife, cut 3 heart or round shapes from the sponge. Keep the trimmings.

Place one piece of sponge on a cake card and, using a palette knife or spatula, spread with a thick layer of the frosting. Top with the next layer of sponge, making sure they are aligned, and spread with more frosting. Add the next layer of sponge and press down gently to level the top. Using a palette knife, mask the outside of the cake with a thin layer of frosting. Put the cake in the fridge for 30 minutes to firm up, then cover with the remaining frosting.

Blitz the cake trimmings to crumbs in a food processor, using the pulse setting. Press the crumbs on to the cake to cover it completely.

57 Rogel Toffee Cake
Argentina

Wow, this cake is for those who have a very sweet tooth! Consisting of crackers layered with dulce de leche and meringue, it's pretty easy to make and looks impressive. Why it's called Rogel I am not too sure.

I find individual cakes easier to serve – it's quite hard to cut a large one, as the crackers are so crisp. Individual cakes mean everyone gets their own to tackle as best they can.

Makes 6

100g unsalted butter
260g plain flour
4 medium eggs, separated
400g dulce de leche
100g icing sugar

Beat the butter and flour together with an electric mixer until the mixture looks like breadcrumbs. Add the egg yolks and a teaspoon of water and mix to a soft but not sticky dough; if it seems too firm, add a little more water. Wrap the dough in cling film and chill for 1 hour.

Heat the oven to 180°C/Gas Mark 4. Roll out the dough extremely thinly on a floured surface – it should be about 0.5mm thick. Cut into 7.5cm circles with a pastry cutter, re-rolling the trimmings to cut out as many circles as possible. Place the circles on a greased baking tray and prick them all over with a fork. Bake for 5–10 minutes, until golden brown and crisp, then remove from the oven and leave to cool on the baking tray.

Warm the dulce de leche in a pan or a microwave so it is a spreadable consistency. Place one of the discs on a serving plate and spread with the dulce de leche. Repeat until you have 5 or 6 layers. Make more cakes with the remaining discs and dulce de leche.

Place the sugar and egg whites in a large bowl set over a pan of simmering water, making sure the water doesn't touch the base of the bowl. Whisk with an electric beater until it forms stiff peaks. Transfer this meringue to a piping bag fitted with a 1cm plain nozzle and pipe little peaks of meringue on top of the cakes. The meringue will crisp up as it dries so there is no need to brown it in the oven, but do colour it with a blowtorch, if you have one. The cakes are best eaten within a few hours to experience all the wonderful textures at their best.

58 Rüebli Carrot Muffins with Kirsch Icing
Switzerland

This light, fluffy carrot cake comes from the Aargau region of Switzerland and often contains ground nuts such as almonds, walnuts or hazelnuts. I bake mine in muffin cases but it works just as well baked in a round 25cm cake tin about 5cm deep. Take the time to make the traditional marzipan carrots; they really brighten up the cakes.

Makes 10

150g carrots, grated
200g ground almonds
135g ground walnuts
50g fresh wholemeal breadcrumbs
½ teaspoon ground nutmeg
1 teaspoon ground cinnamon
1 teaspoon ground ginger
1 teaspoon baking powder
100g candied pineapple, chopped
6 large eggs, separated
280g light soft brown sugar
2 teaspoons grated lemon zest
3 tablespoons kirsch
75g sultanas

Marzipan carrots
100g marzipan
a few drops of green food colouring
a little icing sugar
a few drops of orange food
 colouring

Kirsch icing
1 egg white
150–200g icing sugar
1 tablespoon kirsch
a little lemon juice, if necessary

Heat the oven to 170°C/Gas Mark 3. Line a muffin tin with 10 paper muffin cases.

Place the carrots, ground almonds and ground walnuts into a large mixing bowl, add the breadcrumbs, spices and baking powder and mix to combine. Add the candied pineapple and mix again. In a separate bowl, whisk the egg yolks with a third of the sugar until thick and creamy. Whisk in the remaining sugar, plus the lemon zest and kirsch. Continue whisking for another 2 minutes.

In a very clean, grease-free bowl, whisk the egg whites to stiff peaks. Using a large metal spoon, fold them into the egg yolk mixture, then fold in the dry ingredients a third at a time, being careful not to lose all the volume. Finally, fold in the sultanas. Spoon the mixture into the muffin cases.

Bake for 20–30 minutes, until the cakes spring back when pressed lightly with your finger and a cake skewer inserted in the centre comes out clean. Turn out of the tin on a wire rack to cool.

To make the carrots, pinch off a teaspoon-sized piece of the marzipan and colour it green, using a little icing sugar to prevent it getting sticky. Colour the rest of the marzipan orange. Divide the orange marzipan into 10 pieces and roll them into cones. Mark with the back of a knife so they look like carrots. Pinch very small pieces of the green marzipan and roll into 1cm lengths. Place them on top of the cones and, using a knife, gently press each one in the middle so it curls up to form the top of the carrot.

To make the icing, put the egg white in a bowl, sift in about 75g of the icing sugar and whisk with an electric mixer for about 3 minutes, until smooth. Gradually whisk in another 75g icing sugar and continue whisking until the mixture is thick enough to leave a trail on the surface, adding more icing sugar if necessary. Mix in the kirsch. The icing should be a coating consistency; add a little lemon juice if it seems too thick and a little more icing sugar if it is too thin. Spoon the icing over the muffins and decorate with the carrots.

59

Rum Cake
Barbados

This cake cannot be made in a hurry, as the dried fruit has to be steeped in alcohol for at least a week. I spent some time in Barbados working as a pastry chef at the Sandy Lane resort, where locals and visitors alike loved this recipe. This particular version came from Karen Bailey, a local lass, who worked alongside me in the pastry department and had a natural talent for cake making and decorating. Barbados produces many good dark rums that are ideal for this cake. I have known it to keep in a tin for up to six months; in fact, it only improves with time.

Makes a 30cm cake

250g plain flour
½ teaspoon salt
2 teaspoons baking powder
½ teaspoon ground cinnamon
½ teaspoon ground ginger
1 teaspoon ground mixed spice
¼ teaspoon ground nutmeg
250g unsalted butter
200g dark soft brown sugar
3 large eggs
1 teaspoon vanilla extract
1 teaspoon almond extract
½ teaspoon lemon juice
1 teaspoon grated lime zest
80g almonds, chopped

Dried fruit
120g mixed candied peel, chopped
50g glacé cherries, cut into quarters
160g raisins
160g sultanas
200g currants
80g dates, chopped
80g pitted semi-soft prunes, chopped
375ml dark rum

125ml cherry brandy
1 tablespoon Angostura bitters

Burnt sugar syrup
90g caster sugar
75ml warm water

To soak the cake
60ml dark rum
60ml cherry brandy

Prepare the dried fruit at least one week in advance, preferably two. Place all the fruit in a large bowl. Warm the rum, cherry brandy and Angostura bitters in a pan but do not let them boil. Pour them over the fruit and wrap the bowl tightly in cling film. Leave to soak for at least a week – the longer the better.

To make the burnt sugar syrup, place the sugar in a deep, heavy-based pan and stir over a high heat until it melts and caramelises. Now let it darken until it almost looks burned. Turn off the heat and slowly add the warm water, being very careful not to burn yourself. The caramel will spit and bubble violently. Return the pan to the heat and bring back to the boil so the mixture becomes liquid again.

Heat the oven to 140°C/Gas Mark 1. Grease a 30cm square deep cake tin and double line it with baking parchment.

Sift the flour, salt, baking powder, and spices into a bowl. In a separate bowl, beat the butter and sugar together until pale and fluffy, using an electric mixer. Lightly whisk the eggs, vanilla and almond extract together, then add them to the mixture a little at a time, beating well after each addition. Fold in the flour mixture. Add the lemon juice, lime zest, almonds, the soaked fruit, along with any unabsorbed liquid, and 90ml of the burnt sugar syrup. Mix until just combined. Transfer the mixture to the prepared cake tin.

Place a deep tray of cold water in the bottom of the oven for the first hour of cooking to keep the cake moist. Place the cake in the oven and bake for 2–2½ hours, until a skewer inserted in the centre comes out clean. Remove from the oven, pierce the top all over with a skewer and slowly pour over the rum and cherry brandy, mixed together. Leave to cool in the tin.

This cake should keep for months in an airtight container. Drench with more rum occasionally to moisten.

60

Runeberg Cake
Finland

This cake takes its name from the Finnish poet, Johan Ludvig Runeberg, who supposedly ate one every day for breakfast. I'm not opposed to having cake for breakfast either. It is usually available only from the beginning of January until Runeberg's birthday on 5 February. The cakes are traditionally made in individual dariole moulds but I decided to make one large cake here and fill it with cream. I also like to add some fresh raspberries when they are in season. They make the cake look quite regal and add a little extra tartness.

Makes a 20cm cake

75g amaretti biscuits
110g plain flour
50g ground almonds
50g ground hazelnuts
½ teaspoon baking powder
½ teaspoon bicarbonate of soda
½ teaspoon salt
110g unsalted butter, at room temperature
100g dark muscovado sugar
110g light soft brown sugar
2 medium eggs
½ teaspoon vanilla extract
grated zest of 2 oranges
65ml whole milk
65ml orange juice

Raspberry jam
300g frozen raspberries
150g caster sugar
1 tablespoon lemon juice

Rum syrup
125g caster sugar
125ml water
30ml dark rum

Filling
300ml whipping cream
1 teaspoon vanilla extract
25g icing sugar

To decorate
a little icing sugar
150g white ready-to-roll icing
1 punnet of raspberries (optional)

Heat the oven to 150°C/Gas Mark 2. Grease and flour two 20cm sandwich cake tins.

Place the amaretti in a plastic bag and crush them to a fine powder with a rolling pin. Transfer to a large bowl and stir in the flour, ground almonds and hazelnuts, baking powder, bicarbonate of soda and salt.

Place the butter and both sugars in a mixing bowl and cream together with an electric mixer until pale and fluffy. Lightly whisk the eggs with the vanilla and add to the mixture a little at a time, beating well after each addition. Mix in the grated orange zest. Using a large metal spoon, fold in the dry ingredients alternately with the milk and orange juice. Divide the batter evenly between the cake tins and level the surface.

Bake the cakes for 20–25 minutes, until a skewer inserted in the centre comes out clean. Cool in the tins for 10–15 minutes, then turn out on to a wire rack to cool completely.

To make the raspberry jam, put the raspberries in a pan and heat gently until they start to simmer. Add the sugar and stir to dissolve. Continue to simmer over a low heat for about 10 minutes, until the mixture reaches setting point.

The best way to test for setting point is to drop a small amount of the mix on to a plate that you've chilled thoroughly in the freezer; the mixture should form a skin and set in a matter of 30 seconds or so. When it is ready, stir in the lemon juice and leave to cool.

To make the syrup, put the sugar and water in a small pan and bring to the boil, stirring to dissolve the sugar. Remove from the heat and stir in the rum. Brush the syrup generously over the bottom layer of the cake.

Whisk the cream with the vanilla and icing sugar until it forms firm peaks. Transfer to a piping bag fitted with a St Honoré nozzle. With the open part of the nozzle facing upwards, pipe a short line of the cream about 2.5cm long on the edge of the cake, taking it in towards the centre of the cake slightly, to give the shape shown in the picture. Continue to pipe the cream in the same fashion around the edge of the cake, then fill the centre with more cream. If you don't have a St Honoré piping nozzle, you could just pipe neat blobs with a 2.5cm nozzle.

Soak the second layer of sponge with rum syrup and place it on top of the cream. Spoon the raspberry jam into the centre of the cake, pushing it to within about 1cm of the edge.

On a surface lightly dusted with icing sugar, roll the white icing out into a rope; it should be large enough to fit around the jam on the top of the cake. Arrange it on the cake, then pinch it with crimpers. If using the raspberries, arrange them in a ring inside the rope.

61

Princess Cake
Sweden

In 1930 three cakes were made to honour the three Swedish princesses, Martha, Astrid and Margaretha. However, it was much later that Annika Larsson, a baker at Grillska Konditoriet in Stockholm, combined features from all three cakes to create the modern version of this cake, known as princess cake. The dome-shaped cake is filled with vanilla custard and raspberries, enrobed in green marzipan and topped with a single pink rose. Sometimes there is white chocolate piped on top of the cake as well. It's simply divine, especially if you love marzipan.

Makes a 20cm cake

3 medium eggs
75g caster sugar
75g plain flour, sifted
25g unsalted butter, melted

Vanilla custard
3 egg yolks
75g caster sugar

20g cornflour
1 vanilla pod
250ml whole milk
25g unsalted butter, diced

Filling
250ml double cream
150g raspberries

2 tablespoons raspberry jam

To decorate
350g green marzipan
a little icing sugar
50g white chocolate, melted
100g light pink marzipan

Heat the oven to 180°C/Gas Mark 4. Grease and flour a 20cm dome mould.

Place the eggs and sugar in a large bowl and whisk with an electric mixer until pale, fluffy and trebled in volume. Gently fold in the sifted flour with a large metal spoon, keeping as much volume as possible. Fold in the melted butter.

Sit the dome mould on a 15cm cutter or cake ring so it does not wobble around. Spoon the cake mix into the mould, place in the oven, still on the cutter or cake ring, and bake for 20–25 minutes, until a skewer inserted in the centre comes out clean. Leave to cool in the tin for 10 minutes before turning out on to a wire rack to cool completely.

Next make the vanilla custard. Put the egg yolks, sugar and cornflour into a bowl and mix to a smooth paste. Slit open the vanilla pod lengthwise, put it in a pan with the milk and bring to the boil. Remove the vanilla pod, scrape out the seeds into the milk, then pour the milk over the egg yolk mixture and stir to combine. Return to the pan and whisk continuously over a medium heat until it returns to the boil. Cook for a further minute over a low heat, then remove from the heat, add the butter and stir until melted. Pass through a fine sieve into a bowl. Cover the surface with cling film, leave to cool, then place in the fridge.

Whip the cream to firm peaks and put it in the fridge. Using a serrated knife, cut the cake horizontally into 3 even layers. Lightly whisk the vanilla custard until smooth, then fold the whipped cream into the

vanilla custard.

Set the clean dome mould on the 15cm cutter or cake ring again to prevent it wobbling. Spoon about a quarter of the custard and cream mixture into the mould. Put the dome part of the cake into the tin so it goes down into the custard, pressing gently so the custard comes up around the cake. Spoon some of the raspberries on to the cake.

Place the rest of the custard cream mixture in a piping bag fitted with a 2.5cm plain nozzle and pipe a layer over the sponge and raspberries. Spread the raspberry jam over the second cake layer and place, jam-side down, on the custard cream. Add the remaining raspberries and pipe over more custard cream. Put the third cake layer in the mould, bottom-side up. It should now be level with the top of the mould. Chill the cake, still in the mould, in the freezer for 1 hour.

Sit the mould briefly in a bowl of hot water to loosen the cake. Take care not to overheat the mould or the cream will start to melt. You can also use a blowtorch to warm the outside of the mould, if you have one. Turn the cake out on to a 20cm cake card.

Roll out the green marzipan on a work surface lightly dusted with icing sugar. Roll it up loosely on the rolling pin and lay it over the cake. Tuck it around the cake, trying not to make any folds. Trim off the excess with a small knife. Make a rope out of the excess marzipan and wrap it around the base of the cake. Pinch with crimpers to mark it.

Spoon the melted white chocolate into a small paper piping bag and

cut a small hole in the tip. Pipe a design on top of the cake as shown in the picture or simply zigzag it over the cake.

To make the marzipan rose, divide the pink marzipan into 6–8 walnut-sized balls; these will be the petals. Place one piece of marzipan between 2 sheets of thick cellophane (or thick plastic, such as a sandwich bag) that have been lightly dusted with icing sugar; this will help prevent the marzipan sticking. Start by pushing the marzipan down sideways to make it longer, and then flatten on one side with your thumb until it is very thin. The middle needs to remain thicker. Remove the marzipan from the cellophane and repeat with the other balls.

Take the first petal you made and roll it into a spiral shape to make a cone; this will form the centre of the rose. Wrap the other petals around the cone, overlapping them one at a time. Finally turn back the edges a little to give the rose some movement. I usually end up with a thick base and I pinch this part of the rose off or cut it away with a small knife.

Place the rose on top of the cake and finish with leaves or another small rope made from any leftover green marzipan.

62

Anthills
Lithuania

This cake gets its name, skruzdėlynas, *or anthills, from the poppy seeds that are sprinkled over it and are thought to resemble ants. It is made by stacking fried pastries together and glazing them with honey. They are crisp and crunchy, and much easier to eat than they are to construct. They are also great to snack on without building into a tower. Although the dough is unsweetened, the honey adds all the sweetness you need, plus the stickiness to hold the pastries in place. It needs to be eaten immediately after making, otherwise it will become soggy.*

Pastry
2 medium eggs
½ tablespoon soured cream
250g plain flour
a pinch of salt
200ml sunflower oil

To fry
800ml sunflower or vegetable oil

Honey syrup
6 tablespoons honey
1 teaspoon vanilla extract
2 tablespoons water

To decorate
1 tablespoon poppy seeds

Place the eggs, soured cream, flour, salt and sunflower oil in a freestanding electric mixer fitted with the dough hook and mix to a smooth, soft dough (or you can mix it in a bowl, using a wooden spoon). If it seems sticky, add a little more flour. Wrap the dough in cling film and leave to rest in the fridge for at least 2 hours.

Divide the dough into 3 and roll each piece out on a lightly floured surface as thinly as possible – it should look almost transparent and be as thin as filo pastry. Cut it into 7.5cm triangles; these don't need to be regular shapes. I find it easier to make a few, fry them and then go back to rolling and cutting the rest.

To fry, heat the oil to about 180°C in a large, deep pan. Fry the triangles in batches for about 3 minutes, until golden brown, turning them over frequently as they cook. Lift them from the oil with a slotted spoon and place on kitchen paper.

Once all the pastries have been cooked, make the syrup. Put all the ingredients in a pan, bring to the boil and simmer for 3–4 minutes. Drizzle some of the syrup over a serving dish and start to build up layers of fritters, adding more syrup as glue as you build your tower. Finish by drizzling any remaining syrup over the cake and sprinkling with the poppy seeds. Serve immediately.

63

Pandoro di Verona
Italy

Pandoro *means golden bread, and was originally intended for the Venetian aristocracy, who could afford such luxuries as butter, eggs and honey. Gradually over the years, sugar replaced honey, other changes were made and the recipe developed the soft, cakey texture we know today. In 1894 a man named Domenico Melegatti applied for a patent for a procedure that revolutionised the production of pandoro. I have no idea what the procedure was but I do know that the cake can take master pandoro bakers a full 24 hours to make. Although the version below is not strictly authentic, it makes a lovely cake and takes about 9 hours from start to finish – most of this is rising time rather than hands-on work. You can speed up the proving process by making the kitchen as warm as possible. If you don't have a pandoro tin, use an 18cm round, deep tin instead.*

The icing sugar is supposed to resemble the snowy peaks of the Italian Alps at Christmas, when the cake is normally served.

Makes an 18cm cake

275g plain flour
3 egg yolks
90g caster sugar
25g unsalted butter, melted
60ml water
1 medium egg
grated zest of ½ lemon
icing sugar for dusting

Yeast mixture
30g plain flour
7g easy-blend dried yeast
7g caster sugar
30ml warm water

Put all the ingredients for the yeast mixture in a small bowl and mix well. Cover with a damp tea towel and leave to rise in a warm place for 2 hours or until doubled in size.

Place 165g of the flour in a freestanding electric mixer fitted with a dough hook. In a separate bowl, beat together 2 egg yolks, 60g caster sugar, the butter and water. Add the yeast mixture and mix well. Pour this mixture into the flour and mix on a low speed to form a sticky dough. Continue to work the dough for 5–10 minutes, until smooth. It should remain somewhat tacky, unlike bread dough. Oil or butter a large bowl and put the dough in it, turning to coat all sides. Cover with cling film and leave to rise in a warm place for 2 hours.

Punch down the dough and add the remaining flour, egg yolk and sugar, plus the egg and lemon zest. Knead until blended, then knead by hand on a floured work surface for 10 minutes, until smooth and shiny; if this seems like too much work, you can knock the dough back in the food mixer on a low speed. Place in an oiled or buttered bowl, cover with cling film, then leave to rise for another 2 hours.

Butter and flour a pandoro tin. Punch the dough down and roll it into a ball. Place it in the tin, cover and leave to rise for 1½ hours or until doubled in size.

Heat the oven to 190°C/Gas Mark 5. Bake the cake for 35 minutes, until a skewer inserted in the centre comes out clean. Leave in the tin for 10 minutes, then turn out on to a wire rack to cool completely. Dust liberally with icing sugar.

64

Marmalade Cake
Scotland

In 1797 the Keiller marmalade factory in Dundee adapted an existing recipe for marmalade by adding the characteristic shreds of orange peel, and so commercial marmalade was born. Marmalade cakes are enjoyed to this day in Scotland and many versions exist. I like to decorate mine with an assortment of oranges. If blood oranges are in season, they look attractive; otherwise navel oranges work just as well, as they slice neatly and don't contain pips. You can also use kumquats. If you live in the USA, Cara Cara oranges would make a nice twist to the finish too.

Makes a small loaf

250g self-raising flour
a pinch of salt
125g unsalted butter, diced
125g caster sugar
grated zest of 1 large orange
2 large eggs, lightly beaten
2 tablespoons orange marmalade
2 tablespoons milk
a few drops of vanilla extract

Orange syrup
juice and grated zest of 2 oranges
4 tablespoons icing sugar

To decorate
100g caster sugar
75ml water
1–2 large blood oranges or navel oranges, peeled and thickly sliced
4 tablespoons thick-cut orange marmalade

Heat the oven to 170°C/Gas Mark 3. Grease a 450g loaf tin and line the base and sides with a piece of baking parchment.

Sift the flour and salt into a bowl and rub in the butter until the mixture looks like fine breadcrumbs. Stir in the sugar and orange zest, then gradually add the eggs, marmalade, milk and vanilla, whisking well to achieve the consistency of a thick batter.

Pour into the prepared cake tin and bake for 40 minutes, until the top springs back when pressed gently with your finger and a skewer inserted in the centre comes out clean.

Meanwhile, put all the ingredients for the syrup in a pan, bring to the boil and simmer for 3–4 minutes. When the cake is done, pierce the top with a skewer and pour the syrup over it. Leave to cool in the tin.

To caramelise the oranges for decoration, put the sugar in a heavy-based frying pan, place over a high heat and stir until it turns into a light caramel. Carefully add the water, taking care it doesn't spit out of the pan, and stir over a medium heat until the caramel becomes liquid. Add the orange slices and cook for 2–3 minutes, until they take on the colour and flavour of the caramel, turning them over once. Remove from the pan and leave to cool on a plate.

Mix any remaining caramel with the marmalade. Place in a small pan and bring to the boil, adding a splash of water if you didn't have any excess caramel, so it is runny enough to pour over the cake. Arrange the caramelised orange slices on top of the cake and pour over the hot marmalade.

65

Cinnamon and Ricotta Filo Cake
Turkey

Known as sini katmeri *in Turkey, this unusual filo cake has two very distinct textures: a crisp exterior and a soft, slightly soggy inside, making a delightful combination. It contains a whopping 30g cinnamon but feel free to reduce the amount if you'd rather it were a hint than a dominant flavour. I love nuts so much that I've included pistachio nuts here but you can simply use more almonds if you wish. When researching this cake, I tried several recipes and the finish I liked best was a thin layer of caramel, which adds sweetness to the citrus and ricotta filling. It's best eaten warm if you want to enjoy the crisp filo pastry at its best.*

Makes a 20cm cake

200g pistachios, roughly chopped
400g ground almonds
600g ricotta cheese
600ml condensed milk
30g ground cinnamon
grated zest of 1 lemon
30g caster sugar
80g unsalted butter, melted
1 packet of filo pastry

Rose syrup
250g caster sugar
250ml water
a few drops of rosewater

Caramel topping
100g caster sugar
80ml water

To decorate
1 teaspoon pistachio nuts, chopped
30g whole almonds, toasted

Heat the oven to 180°C/Gas Mark 4. Put the pistachio nuts and ground almonds in a bowl, mix in the ricotta cheese, then slowly add about half the condensed milk until the mixture forms a thick paste. Mix in the cinnamon, lemon zest and sugar.

Grease a 20cm springform cake tin with a little of the melted butter. Cut 5–6 sheets of filo pastry into strips approximately 7.5cm wide and brush them lightly with the remaining condensed milk. Line the tin with the strips so they are overlapping to cover the base and sides completely, then brush with melted butter. It doesn't matter if the filo overhangs the edge of the tin a little. Keep the remaining pastry from drying out while you do this by rolling it back up in cling film.

Fill the lined tin with the ricotta and nut mixture, pressing it down lightly to level the top. Fold any overhanging bits of pastry over the filling. Cut 2 more sheets of filo into random pieces and lay them at angles on top of the cake, covering the entire surface and using the condensed milk as glue. It's okay if they don't all look perfect; they will look great when cooked. Brush the top with the remaining melted butter.

Bake for 25–30 minutes, until golden and crisp. Meanwhile, make the syrup. Put the sugar and water in a pan, bring to the boil, stirring to dissolve the sugar, and boil for 2–3 minutes to make a syrup. Remove from the heat and add the rosewater. When the cake comes out of the oven, let it stand for 5 minutes and then pour the hot syrup over it. Leave for another 5 minutes, then remove from the tin.

To make the caramel topping, put the sugar and 50ml of the water into a pan, bring to the boil, stirring to dissolve the sugar, then boil until it becomes a light golden caramel. Remove from the heat and slowly add the remaining 30ml water, being very careful as it will spit and can burn you. Bring the caramel back to the boil and then pour it over the warm cake, letting it drizzle down the sides. Sprinkle with the chopped pistachio nuts and toasted almonds. Serve warm, with vanilla ice cream.

66

Spiral Pandan Moon Cakes
China

The moon is always at its brightest on the fifteenth day of the eighth month of the lunar calendar. In China this day is known as the Festival of the Moon, or Mid-Autumn Festival – and, of course, it would not be a festival without food and dance. The moon cake celebrates this special day. It is often filled with lotus seed paste, red beans and the traditional salty egg yolk. My version is filled with sweet potato. These little individual cakes need quite a lot of attention, as you have to fold and roll two doughs to create a flaky pastry. However, if you work through the recipe step by step, you should be delighted with the results. Pandan essence is available online or in Asian shops.

Makes 16

Moon cake filling
500g sweet potatoes, peeled and cut into 5cm chunks (you need 300g cooked weight)
55ml whole milk
50g unsalted butter
50g caster sugar
½ teaspoon salt

Water dough
200g plain flour
30g icing sugar
a pinch of salt
80g cold unsalted butter, cut into 2.5cm cubes
80ml water

Oil dough
180g plain flour
a pinch of salt
90ml vegetable oil
½ teaspoon pandan essence

First make the filling. Cook the sweet potatoes in boiling water until tender, then drain thoroughly. Mash the potatoes, then add the rest of the ingredients for the filling and mix to a stiff paste.

To make the water dough, sift the flour, icing sugar and salt together, add the butter and mix on a low speed with an electric mixer until the mixture resembles breadcrumbs (you could also rub the butter in by hand, like making pastry). Add the water and mix to a soft dough. If it is sticky, add a little more flour. Cover and leave to rest in the fridge for 30 minutes.

To make the oil dough, sift the flour and salt into a mixing bowl, make a well in the centre and add the oil and pandan essence. Draw in the flour from the sides and mix to form a soft, even-coloured dough. Do not over mix. It is very important that the dough is the same consistency as the water dough. Cover and leave to rest in the fridge for 30 minutes.

Heat the oven to 180°C/Gas Mark 4. Divide each dough in half. For the water dough, shape each half into a 15cm x 7.5cm rectangle. Flatten each piece of oil dough into a rectangle 2.5cm smaller than the water dough all round. Fold each piece of water dough around a piece of oil dough to wrap it like a parcel. Pinch to seal the edges.

On a lightly floured surface, roll each block, sealed-side facing up, into a rectangle about 40cm long and 10cm wide. Roll up from a short side into a log, as you would a Swiss roll. Turn the roll 90 degrees, roll it out again to the same size and roll up again.

Using a sharp knife or a pastry cutter, cut each log into 8 equal pieces. They should now look like pinwheels. Take care not to tear the dough or squash the layers together. With the cut side facing down, flatten the dough, making the edges slightly thinner than the centre. Divide the sweet potato filling into 16 balls and put one on each circle of dough. Bring up the sides to make a ball, then pinch to seal, taking care not to pull too hard or you will tear the layers.

Place the cakes sealed-side down on a baking tray lined with baking parchment and bake for about 30 minutes, until the top and bottom are a light golden brown. They are good served warm or cold.

67 Steamed Chocolate and Strawberry Zebra Cake
Indonesia

Steamed cakes are very popular in Indonesia. I plumped for a zebra effect for this one but it can be coloured and flavoured as you wish. If the 3-hour cooking time puts you off, you can make small cakes in dariole moulds or pudding cups and steam them for just 45 minutes.

This is a fabulous way to use up leftover egg whites. The recipe does call for 14, though, which I appreciate is a lot. You could use pasteurised egg whites, available in cartons from large supermarkets, if the thought of using 14 egg yolks for something else is too daunting.

The strawberry apple sprinkles are made by Whitworth and stocked by most large supermarkets.

Makes a 23cm cake

170g plain flour
2 teaspoons baking powder
450ml egg whites (about 14)
225g caster sugar
a pinch of salt
2 teaspoons lemon juice
175ml vegetable oil
1 teaspoon vanilla extract
1 tablespoon milk (optional)
10g cocoa powder
2 x 10g tubes of black food gel colouring
a few drops of strawberry flavouring (see page 188)
50g strawberry apple sprinkles, plus a few extra to decorate
a little icing sugar

Heat 5cm water in a large steamer or, if you don't have one large enough to hold a 23cm cake tin, a large pan with an upturned tin or metal plate in the base. Grease a 23cm round cake tin (not a loose-based one), about 7.5cm deep.

Sift the flour and baking powder together. Put the egg whites in a very large bowl with a third of the sugar. Using an electric mixer, whisk on high speed until they start to form peaks, then add another third of the sugar and continue to whisk on high. Once stiff peaks have formed, add the remaining sugar, plus the salt and lemon juice, and whisk for a further minute, until firm. Fold in the flour with a large metal spoon, taking care not to lose the volume. Fold in the oil and vanilla. The mixture should be a thick batter; if it seems a little too thick, add the milk.

Transfer half the mixture to another bowl. Mix in the cocoa powder and black food colouring, then transfer the mixture to a jug. Add the strawberry flavouring and strawberry apple pieces to the remaining mixture and transfer to a second jug.

Pour the brown batter into the centre of the prepared cake tin, creating a circle about 10cm in diameter; it will spread out to the sides as you add more batter. Next pour the white batter into the centre of the brown batter, in a circle about 7.5cm in diameter. Keep alternating between white and brown batter until they are both used up. Cover the top of the tin with lightly greased greaseproof paper and secure with string. Wrap the top in foil, tucking it under the lip of the tin.

Place in the steamer, or in the pan of water on the upturned tin or plate. Steam for 2½–3 hours, topping up the water as necessary, until the cake is firm to the touch and a skewer inserted in the centre comes out clean (you will have to unwrap it to check). Lift the cake out of the steamer using oven gloves. Leave for 10 minutes, then remove from the tin and leave to cool. Finish with a dusting of icing sugar and sprinkle over a few strawberry apple pieces.

68

Strawberry Marshmallow Angel Cake
USA

With its light, fluffy, white texture, angel cake really lives up to its name. It has African–American roots and was often offered at funeral teas. Traditionally this cake is baked in a tin designed especially for the purpose, although a bundt tin can also be used. It is very important not to grease the tin, or the cake will fall and become shallow and tough. Once it is baked, it has to be inverted straight away, so the texture remains light whilst cooling.

I could not resist pimping my cake – it cried out for decoration. The strawberries help introduce texture and sweetness to this lovely, soft, airy confection....

Makes a 25cm cake

300g caster sugar
150g plain flour
375ml egg whites (about 11)
1 tablespoon lemon juice
1 teaspoon cream of tartar
½ teaspoon salt
2 teaspoons vanilla extract

Frosting

2 tablespoons condensed milk
250g full-fat cream cheese
3 tablespoons puréed strawberries
300ml whipping cream
1 tablespoon Cointreau or orange liqueur (optional)
1 teaspoon vanilla extract

Filling

4 tablespoons strawberry jam

To decorate

250g pink and white mini marshmallows
a little icing sugar
250g strawberries, hulled and cut into quarters
50ml bought strawberry sauce or puréed strawberries

Heat the oven to 150°C/Gas Mark 2. Mix half the sugar with the flour and sift into a bowl. Put the egg whites and the remaining sugar into a very large, grease-free bowl and, using an electric mixer, whisk on high speed until they form medium peaks. Add the lemon juice, cream of tartar, salt and vanilla and continue to whisk until the meringue is glossy and forms firm peaks. Carefully fold in the dry ingredients with a large metal spoon, trying to lose as little volume as possible. Spoon into a 25cm angel food cake tin – remember, the tin should not be greased first.

Bake for 40–45 minutes, until the cake springs back when pressed lightly with your finger and a skewer inserted in the centre comes out clean. Invert the cake on to a bottle and let it cool upside down – make sure you have balanced it evenly. When it is completely cold, remove the cake from the tin.

Combine all the ingredients for the frosting in a bowl and whisk until smooth and creamy. Cut the cake into 3 layers. Place the bottom layer on a cake card or serving plate and spread with half the strawberry jam, followed by a layer of frosting. Add the second cake layer and spread with the remaining jam and another layer of frosting. Place the remaining piece of cake on top. Using a palette knife or spatula, completely cover the outside of the cake with the remaining frosting.

Press the mini marshmallows around the base of the cake. Dust with icing sugar, then decorate the top with the cut strawberries and drizzle with the strawberry sauce.

69

Treacle Scones
Scotland

The original scone was an unleavened round about 20cm in diameter, baked on a griddle and then cut into wedges. The simplest of teatime treats, these treacle scones have a molasses flavour and a kick from both ground and candied ginger. Delightful warm with butter and Scottish marmalade, they are perfect for a cold winter teatime – or even a summer picnic.

Makes 8

225g self-raising flour
50g caster sugar
½ teaspoon baking powder
2 teaspoons ground ginger
50g unsalted butter, diced
40g candied stem ginger, finely chopped
30g sultanas
1 rounded tablespoon black treacle (about 35g)
90ml milk
1 egg yolk, beaten with 1 tablespoon milk, to glaze

Heat the oven to 190°C/Gas Mark 5. Line a baking tray with baking parchment.

Sift the flour, caster sugar, baking powder and ground ginger into a large bowl. Add the butter and rub it in with your fingertips until the mixture looks like fine breadcrumbs. Stir in the chopped ginger and sultanas. Mix the treacle with the milk, add to the dry ingredients and bring together to form a soft but not sticky dough. Add a little more milk if it seems too dry. (You can do the entire process in an electric mixer fitted with the paddle attachment, if you wish.)

Turn the mixture out on to a lightly floured surface and knead gently for 3–4 minutes, until soft and elastic. Roll out to 2.5cm thick and cut into rounds with a 5cm cutter. Place on the lined baking tray. Brush the tops of the scones with the beaten egg yolk. Leave in a warm place for 20–30 minutes, until doubled in size, then brush the tops with the glaze again.

Bake for 10–12 minutes. The best way to tell if the scones are done is to take one from the centre of the tray and pull it open to check the dough is cooked in the middle. Transfer to a wire rack to cool.

70 Swiss Roll
England

Despite its name, the Swiss roll has no connection with Switzerland. The Americans, who refer to it as a jelly roll, have tried to lay claim to being the first country of aspiring bakers to roll a cake. However, it's more likely it was we Brits, as it first appeared in cookbooks at the same time as the Victoria sandwich and the Battenberg cake. The first recorded reference to a Swiss roll was on a UK steam liner in 1871.

As if to prove a point, it remains a national favourite to this day. I decorated mine with pretty sugarpaste flowers. There are so many available to buy, you will be spoilt for choice.

4 eggs
125g caster sugar, plus extra for
    sprinkling
grated zest of 1 lemon
80g plain flour

Filling
250ml whipping cream
1 teaspoon vanilla extract
10g icing sugar
6 tablespoons strawberry jam

To decorate
icing sugar
ready-made sugarpaste flowers

Heat the oven to 190°C/Gas Mark 5. Lightly grease a 35 x 25cm Swiss roll tin and line it with baking parchment.

Put the eggs and caster sugar in a large bowl set over a pan of gently simmering water, making sure the water doesn't touch the base of the bowl. Using an electric mixer, whisk until they are light, fluffy and trebled in volume. Remove the bowl from the pan of water. Fold in the lemon zest. Sift the flour, sprinkle about a third at a time over the cake mix and fold it in using a large metal spoon. Pour the mixture gently into the prepared Swiss roll tin and level the surface with a spatula.

Bake for 8–10 minutes, until the centre of the cake is slightly springy to the touch and the edges have shrunk away a little from the sides of the tin. While the cake is in the oven, cut a piece of baking parchment slightly larger than the Swiss roll tin and sprinkle it evenly with caster sugar. When the cake is done, invert the Swiss roll on to the sugared paper and carefully lift off the tin. Place a slightly damp tea towel over the cake and leave to cool.

Whip the cream with the vanilla and icing sugar until it forms firm peaks. When the cake is cool, carefully peel off the backing paper, then spread the jam over the sponge. Spread the whipped cream on top in an even layer, reserving a little to decorate. With a long side of the cake nearest you, roll up the Swiss roll away from you, using the paper underneath to help shape it into a neat roll. Move the roll so it is in the centre of the paper. Use the flat side of a large kitchen knife to press down on the top layer of paper. Hold on to the bottom piece of the paper under the roll whilst gently pressing the knife up against the roll to tighten it, moving it up and down the whole length of the roll.

Put the reserved cream in a disposable piping bag, cut a 2.5cm hole in the tip and pipe it in a line along the top of the Swiss roll. Dust with icing sugar, trim off the edges of the roll, then decorate with the sugarpaste flowers. To serve, cut into slices with a warmed knife.

71

Fig and Sesame Honey Drizzle Cake
Turkey

My favourite figs are the sweet, plump, purple-black Turkish ones, which are readily available in September and October. This cake contains sesame seeds, which are also plentiful in Turkey. They give a slight crunch to the outside of the cake, while the fine semolina adds a soft, spongy texture. It's delicious warm but also keeps really well and is equally delightful cold.

Serve with a cup of Turkish coffee.

Makes a 20cm cake

2 tablespoons sesame seeds
200g ground almonds
85g fine semolina
5 eggs, separated
grated zest of 1 lemon
140g icing sugar
50g unsalted butter, melted
4 fresh black figs

Syrup
200g honey
50ml water

Heat the oven to 180°C/Gas Mark 4. Grease a 20cm deep cake tin and sprinkle the base and sides with the sesame seeds.

Mix the almonds and semolina together, rubbing them thoroughly with your fingertips to remove any lumps. Put the egg yolks, lemon zest and 100g of the icing sugar in a bowl and whisk with an electric mixer until pale, fluffy and doubled in volume. In a separate bowl, whisk the egg whites with the remaining icing sugar until they form stiff peaks. Gently fold the egg whites into the egg yolk mix with a large metal spoon, alternating it with the almonds and semolina. Finally, fold in the melted butter.

Transfer the mixture to the prepared tin. Cut the figs in half and arrange on top of the cake. Bake for 20–25 minutes, until firm to the touch.

Remove the cake from the oven and poke small holes into the top with a skewer. Bring the honey and water to the boil to make a syrup and pour it over the warm cake while it is still in the tin. Leave for 10 minutes, then remove from the tin and cool on a wire rack.

72

Pavlova
New Zealand

Both New Zealand and Australia claim to have invented this dessert. According to a biographer of Anna Pavlova, the Russian ballet dancer, it was created for her at a hotel in Wellington during a 1926 ballet tour. Since then it has become one of the world's most fancied desserts. There are hundreds of variations on the recipe and this particular one is for small pavlovas. I make them big enough for two to share but you can pipe them individually if you prefer. Use whatever fruit is in season and change the sauce to complement the fruit if necessary. The sauce below works with most fruits, except kiwi, pineapple, citrus fruits and rhubarb.

Makes 3, each serving 2

120ml egg whites (about 4)
½ teaspoon cream of tartar
240g caster sugar

Raspberry sauce
200g raspberries
300g icing sugar
a little lemon juice

To decorate
600ml double cream
1 teaspoon vanilla extract
50g icing sugar
500g fresh seasonal fruit, cut into
    pieces if necessary

Heat the oven to 120°C/Gas Mark ½. Line a baking sheet with baking parchment.

Put the egg whites in a very clean, grease-free bowl, add the cream of tartar and a third of the sugar and whisk with an electric mixer on high speed until soft peaks form. Gradually add another third of the sugar, whisking on a low speed. Increase the speed to medium and whisk until the meringue is glossy and holding firm peaks. Add the last third of the sugar and whisk until firm and glossy.

Spoon the meringue into a piping bag fitted with a 2.5cm plain nozzle and pipe a dome about 10cm in diameter on the parchment-lined baking sheet. Repeat twice to make 3 domes, spacing them at least 5cm apart, as they will swell in the oven. Bake for 30–40 minutes. When they are ready, you should be able to pick up the meringue domes from the paper without them breaking. The middles should still be a little soft and chewy and the outside a crisp shell. Leave to cool on the trays. Take care whilst handling them, as they will remain fragile.

Blitz the raspberries and icing sugar together in a blender, then strain through a sieve to remove the seeds. Add a little lemon juice to adjust the sweetness – the lemon will also brighten the colour of the sauce. Whisk the cream with the vanilla and icing sugar until it forms stiff peaks.

To assemble, pipe a layer of cream the same diameter as the bottom of the pavlovas on to the centre of a serving dish. Sit a pavlova on top of the cream and surround with the prepared fruit. Repeat with the remaining pavlovas. Pour the sauce over the meringue so it runs down over the fruits. Serve immediately.

73

Vinarterta
Iceland

This Icelandic Christmas cake dates back to the nineteenth century and consists of layers of biscuit sandwiched together with an Armagnac-laden prune jam and topped with waves of butter icing. The dough needs to be rolled out on baking parchment and chilled before you try to handle it, as the sheets are thin and delicate.

Note that the cake has to rest in the fridge for 24 hours after assembly, before it is ready to eat. The filling can be made up to a week in advance and stored in the fridge.

55g unsalted butter
170g caster sugar
1 medium egg, lightly beaten
1 teaspoon vanilla extract
125ml milk
330g plain flour, plus 85–100g for kneading
¼ teaspoon salt
3 teaspoons baking powder
½ teaspoon ground cardamom

Prune jam
500g pitted prunes, chopped
250ml water
25ml Armagnac or brandy
juice of ½ lemon
1 teaspoon ground cardamom

Icing
220g icing sugar, sifted
40g unsalted butter, melted
2 tablespoons milk
1 teaspoon almond extract

Using an electric mixer, cream the butter and sugar together until light and fluffy. Add the egg a little at a time, beating well after each addition. Mix the vanilla with the milk. Sift together the flour, salt, baking powder and cardamom. Fold them into the creamed mixture with a large metal spoon, alternating with the milk and vanilla.

Turn the dough out on to a well-floured surface; it will be soft and slightly sticky. Using the 85–100g flour for kneading, work it gradually into the dough until it is still soft but no longer sticky. Divide the dough in half and roll out one piece thinly between 2 sheets of baking parchment until it is the size of a 35cm x 25cm baking tray. Repeat with the other piece of dough, for which you will need a second baking tray. Place the dough, still between the sheets of paper, in the fridge for 40 minutes.

Meanwhile, make the prune jam. Place the prunes in a pan with the water and cook over a medium heat until they are soft and have absorbed the water. When the mixture starts to look like a paste, stir frequently to prevent it sticking. Add the Armagnac or brandy and continue to cook until it has been absorbed by the prunes. Remove from the heat, stir in the lemon juice and ground cardamom and leave to cool.

Heat the oven to 180°C/Gas Mark 4. Once the dough is firm enough to handle, remove the top sheet of paper from both pieces. Grease the baking trays and turn the dough over on to them, then remove the remaining pieces of paper. Bake for 8–10 minutes; the dough won't colour much but should be firm to the touch. As soon as it comes out of the oven, cut each sheet of dough into 3 equal pieces, using a sharp knife and a ruler. Leave them in the tray to cool, then turn them out and layer them with the prune filling.

To make the icing, put all the ingredients in a bowl and whisk with an electric mixer for about 10 minutes, until they have a fluffy consistency. If it is too stiff, add a little more milk. Spread the icing over the top of the cake and rough it up to look like snow.

Now you have to pop the cake in the fridge and wait patiently for 24 hours while the filling softens the cake. Believe me, it's worth the wait. Trim off the edges before serving. The cake will keep in an airtight container for 2 weeks.

74

Victoria Sandwich Cake
England

One of Queen Victoria's ladies-in-waiting, the Duchess of Bedford, is credited with the invention of 'teatime'. This simple sponge cake was the Queen's favourite. She would often spend time alone at Osborne House on the Isle of Wight, and it is said to be here that the cake was given her name. It is very simple to make and best eaten on the day, sandwiched together with jam or lemon curd, or with cream and seasonal fruit.

Makes an 18cm cake

340g unsalted butter, at room temperature
340g caster sugar
6 large eggs, lightly beaten
340g self-raising flour
2 teaspoons baking powder

Filling
600ml double cream
50g icing sugar, plus extra for dusting
1 teaspoon vanilla extract
6 tablespoons strawberry jam
600g strawberries, hulled

Heat the oven to 180°C/Gas Mark 4. Grease three 18cm sandwich tins and line the bases with baking parchment. Grease them again and dust with flour.

Cream the butter and sugar together with an electric mixer on a medium-high speed until light and fluffy. Add the eggs a little at a time, beating well after each addition. Sift the flour and baking powder together and fold them into the mixture with a large metal spoon.

Divide the mixture equally between the prepared cake tins and level the surface with a palette knife or spatula. Bake for 20–30 minutes, until the cakes have shrunk away from the side of the tins a little and the tops spring back when lightly pressed with your finger. Cool in the tins for a couple of minutes, then loosen the edges with a knife and turn out on to a wire rack to cool completely.

Whip the cream with the icing sugar and vanilla to medium peaks. Place one of the cakes on a cake card or plate and peel away the paper from the base. Spread with half the jam, then cover with a little of the cream. Place a third of the remaining cream in a piping bag fitted with a plain 1cm nozzle and pipe some blobs randomly around the edge of the cake. Trim some of the strawberries so they are all the same height. Arrange them between the blobs of cream, trimmed-side down. Chop 5 strawberries and drop them on to the centre of the cake. Cover with cream, using a spatula so the cream is now level with the top of the upright strawberries. Place the next layer of sponge on top and repeat with the remaining jam, cream and strawberries. Top with the final layer of sponge and press down gently to level the cake. Dust lightly with a little icing sugar and top with a couple of extra strawberries, if liked.

75 Welsh Cakes
Wales

These tasty little griddle cakes are like a cross between a pancake and a scone. They freeze really well and can be easily reheated under the grill. Don't have the pan too hot when cooking them or they will brown too much before they are done in the centre – gently does it, turning them over as they cook to colour both sides. This recipe is from my Welsh friend, John 'the pirate', who made them for me one winter afternoon at a hotel where we worked. It doesn't get much better than having Welsh cakes made for you by a Welshman.

Makes 16

225g plain flour
½ teaspoon baking powder
90g caster sugar, plus extra for
　　sprinkling
½ teaspoon ground mixed spice
50g unsalted butter, diced
50g lard, diced
50g currants
1 medium egg, lightly beaten
2 teaspoons milk, if needed

Place all the dry ingredients in a bowl. Add the butter and lard and rub in with your fingertips until the mixture resembles fine breadcrumbs. Stir in the currants, then mix in the eggs, adding the milk if the mixture seems a little dry. Bring it together to form a soft but not sticky dough.

Roll out on a lightly floured surface to 5mm thick and cut into rounds with a 5cm crinkled cutter.

Grease a heavy-based frying pan or flat griddle with a little lard or oil and place over a medium heat. When it is hot, cook the cakes, in batches, for about 3 minutes, until coloured underneath. Flip them over and cook for a further 3 minutes until coloured on the second side and cooked all the way through. Drain on kitchen paper and sprinkle with caster sugar. Serve immediately, with butter (preferably Welsh) and jam.

76

Zuger Kirschtorte
Switzerland

This cake always reminds me of the Intercontinental Hotel on London's Park Lane, where I worked under Ernst Bachmann, my Swiss mentor. We used to make 12 of these at a time. I think they featured on our menu so that there would be a steady stream of kirsch available for Chef's coffee! Layers of crisp hazelnut meringue encase a kirsch-drenched sponge. Masking the cake with the buttercream takes some skill but the more you practise, the easier it gets.

Makes a 20cm cake

Almond meringue
4 egg whites
120g icing sugar
100g ground almonds
20g cornflour

Cake
3 medium eggs
125g caster sugar
125g plain flour, sifted
25g unsalted butter, melted

Kirsch syrup
60g caster sugar
60ml water
120ml kirsch

Buttercream
150g unsalted butter, softened
150g icing sugar, sifted
1 tablespoon seedless raspberry jam
a few drops of pink food colouring.

To decorate
50–75g dark chocolate (70 per cent cocoa solids), melted
100g flaked almonds or hazelnuts, toasted
2 tablespoons icing sugar

First make the meringue. Heat the oven to 170°C/Gas Mark 3. Line a baking sheet with a piece of baking parchment and, using a 20cm cake ring or tin as a template, draw 2 circles on it about 3cm apart. Grease the paper with a little oil.

Using an electric mixer, whisk the egg whites to stiff peaks with 2 tablespoons of the icing sugar. Sift the remaining icing sugar with the ground almonds and cornflour. Using a large metal spoon, fold the dry ingredients into the beaten egg whites a third at a time, being careful not to over mix or lose volume. Put the mixture in a piping bag fitted with a 5mm nozzle and pipe it on to the circles on the baking parchment to cover them completely; or you can just spread it on with a spoon. Bake for 40–50 minutes, until the meringue is crisp and golden. As soon as you remove the discs from the oven stamp them with the cake ring to make uniform circles. If you are using a springform cake tin, place it over the discs and cut round it with a small, sharp knife while the meringue is still hot. It will firm up and crisp even more when cold. Leave to cool on the tray, then peel off the paper.

To make the cake, grease a 20cm cake tin, line the base with baking parchment and then dust with flour. Using an electric mixer, whisk the eggs and sugar until pale, thick and tripled in volume. Fold in the sifted flour, using a large metal spoon, then fold in the melted butter. Transfer the mixture to the prepared tin and bake at 170°C/Gas Mark 3 for 25–30 minutes, until the sponge springs back when pressed gently

with your finger and a cake skewer inserted in the centre comes out clean. Leave the cake in the tin for 10 minutes, then turn out on to a wire rack to cool.

While the cake is cooling, make the syrup. Put the sugar and water in a small pan and bring to the boil, stirring to dissolve the sugar. Remove from the heat and set aside to cool. Stir in the kirsch.

Now make the buttercream. Make sure the butter is soft and squidgy. Put it in a bowl with the icing sugar and beat with an electric mixer for at least 5 minutes, until pale and fluffy. Mix in the seedless raspberry jam, followed by enough food colouring to give a light pink colour.

To assemble the cake, place one of the meringue discs on a cake card. Brush it with half the melted chocolate and leave to set. Spread with an even layer of buttercream. Place the sponge cake on top and, using a pastry brush, soak it liberally with the kirsch syrup, being sure to use it all.

Brush the other meringue disc with the remaining melted chocolate and cover with a layer of buttercream. Invert it on top of the cake and press down gently to level it. Spread the remaining buttercream over the top and sides of the cake and smooth with a palette knife.

Coat the sides of the cake with the toasted flaked almonds, then place in the fridge for 10 minutes to firm up. Dust the top of the cake with the icing sugar and use the back of a long-bladed knife to make a crisscross pattern on top. The cake is best served at room temperature.

Kiev Cake
Ukraine

This cake was invented at the Karl Marx Confectionery factory in 1956 and has become a symbol of Kiev city, available in all the cafés, restaurants and bars. It always features the same chestnut-leaf design on top, taken from Kiev's informal coat of arms. Completely gluten free, it consists of layers of hazelnut meringue, hazelnut cake, buttercream, apricot jam and a hazelnut chocolate filling and icing. It involves a lot of work and some piping skills but the combination of textures and the rich hazelnut flavour are worth the effort. Be warned: it does get a little messy. If decorating the top seems insurmountable, simply cover it with the buttercream and sprinkle more flaked hazelnuts on top – it will still be delicious.

Makes a 20cm cake

Hazelnut sponge
6 large eggs, separated
100g caster sugar
90g ground almonds
230g ground hazelnuts
1 teaspoon vanilla extract

Meringue
6 large egg whites, at room
   temperature
300g caster sugar
80g hazelnuts, finely chopped

Filling
4 tablespoons apricot jam
4 tablespoons chocolate hazelnut
   spread

Buttercream
300g caster sugar
100ml water

5 egg whites
500g softened unsalted butter, cut
   into 2.5cm cubes

Frosting
440ml dulce de leche
100g dark chocolate (70 per cent
   cocoa solids), melted

To decorate
50g white chocolate, melted
yellow, green, pink and blue food
   colourings
150g hazelnuts, toasted and finely
   chopped

Heat the oven to 170°C/Gas Mark 3. Grease a 20cm springform cake tin and line the base with baking parchment.

Using an electric mixer, beat the egg yolks with 50g of the sugar for 3–4 minutes, until pale and creamy. In a separate bowl, using a clean beater, whisk the egg whites with the remaining sugar until they form stiff peaks. Using a large metal spoon, fold the almonds and hazelnuts into the egg yolk mixture, alternating them with the egg whites. Fold in the vanilla extract.

Spoon into the prepared tin and level the top. Bake for 35 minutes, until the cake is golden brown and springs back when pressed lightly with your finger. Leave to cool in the tin for 10 minutes, then turn out on to a wire rack to cool completely.

Next make the meringue. Heat the oven to 120°C/Gas Mark ½. Wash and dry the tin you used for the cake, line the base with baking parchment and grease the tin and paper with a little oil. Put the egg whites in a large bowl with half the

sugar and whisk on high speed until they form firm peaks. Add the remaining sugar and continue whisking until the meringue is thick and glossy. Fold in the hazelnuts with a large metal spoon. Transfer the mixture to the prepared tin and bake for 1–1½ hours, until the top is light brown but the meringue is still soft in the centre. Leave in the tin to cool.

Cut the cake horizontally in half. Place the bottom layer on a cake card and spread evenly with half the apricot jam, followed by half the chocolate hazelnut spread (it's easier if you warm the spread slightly in a microwave first). Turn the hazelnut meringue out of the tin and place on top of the sponge. This is a bit messy and crumbs from the side of the meringue do tend to drop off. Don't be put off by this. Spread the remaining piece of sponge with the remaining apricot jam and chocolate hazelnut spread, invert it on top of the meringue and press down gently to level the cake. Place in the fridge to firm up.

Meanwhile, make the buttercream. Put 250g of the sugar in a deep, heavy-based pan with the water and mix well to combine. Wash down the sides of the pan with a pastry brush dipped in cold water to remove sugar crystals. Place a sugar thermometer in the pan and then bring to the boil, without stirring, over a high heat. Cook until the sugar thermometer registers 118°C. Meanwhile, put the egg whites and the remaining sugar in a freestanding electric mixer and whisk on medium speed. As soon as the sugar syrup reaches the correct temperature,

remove it from the heat and pour in a slow trickle on to the egg whites, whisking on low speed. Once all the syrup has been added, turn up the speed and whisk until the meringue is thick and has cooled to hand hot. Reduce the speed to low and add the soft butter a cube or two at a time, whisking well after each addition to made a smooth, shiny buttercream.

To make the frosting, beat the dulce de leche and melted chocolate with 350g of the buttercream until smooth and light. Using a spatula or palette knife cover the outside of the cake with the frosting. Place the remaining frosting in a piping bag fitted with a 5mm star piping nozzle and set aside.

Place the melted white chocolate in a small piping bag and cut a small hole in the tip. Zigzag it over the top of the cake to create a trellis effect.

Divide the remaining buttercream between 4 bowls and colour with the food colourings listed. Place the yellow buttercream in a piping bag fitted with a small flower piping nozzle, the green in a bag fitted with a small leaf nozzle, the pink in a bag fitted with a 5mm star piping tip and the blue also in a bag fitted with a 5mm star piping tip. Copy the design for the top of the cake as shown in the photo. Lastly pipe the remaining frosting with the star nozzle around the edge of the cake as shown. Press the chopped hazelnuts on to the sides of the cake.

78 Turrón de Doña Pepa
Peru

This cake is completely crazy. It is actually more like lots of cookies, stuck together with aniseed syrup, and it tastes as amazing as it looks. When I was making it for the first time, it seemed such an odd combination that I didn't expect to like it at all. I could not have been more wrong. It is made to celebrate the month of October, also known as *el Mes Morado*, or purple month, in honour of *el Señor de los Milagros*, the lord of miracles. Everyone wears purple as a sign of respect for the lord of purple, who in return grants them their wishes – which must, of course, be for the good of others. Processions take place all over Lima and this cake can be bought at every street corner and in every shop, although many people choose to bake it themselves.

Makes a 20cm cake

825g plain flour
375g unsalted butter
5 egg yolks
1½ teaspoons salt

Aniseed water
125ml water
1 tablespoon aniseed

Syrup
400g light soft brown sugar
1 litre water
10g liquid glucose
grated zest of 1 orange
5g ground cloves
15g ground mixed spice
15g ground aniseed

To decorate
1 tablespoon multicoloured sprinkles
1 tablespoon hundreds and
    thousands
an assortment of sweets (optional)

First make the aniseed water. Put the water and seeds in a pan, bring to the boil and then remove from the heat. Leave to infuse for 30 minutes, then strain.

Heat the oven to 170°C/Gas Mark 3. Grease a 20cm square loose-bottomed cake tin and line it with a double layer of baking parchment: lay one piece of parchment one way, making sure the ends overhang the tin by 2–3cm, and the other sheet on top the other way, making sure it too overhangs. Grease well.

Place all the ingredients for the cake in a freestanding electric mixer fitted with the paddle attachment, add the aniseed water and mix on a low speed to form a dough. Turn the dough out on to a lightly floured surface and roll it into sticks 1.2cm wide and a little longer than the cake tin. Place them on lightly greased baking trays, spacing them at least 4cm apart. You will need about 25 sticks, which allows for a few spares. Bake for 35–40 minutes, until golden brown. As soon as they come out of the oven, trim the ends off the sticks to neaten them; they should be about 20cm long, so they will fit in the tin. Leave to cool on the trays.

Lay a neat layer of the sticks in the prepared tin to cover the base, then make the syrup. Place all the ingredients in a pan, bring to the boil and simmer for about 20 minutes, until thick and sticky. It should resemble a thick sludge but still be pourable. Pour a layer of the syrup over the cake sticks in the tin. Lay another layer of sticks on top facing the other way and pour over more syrup. Repeat with a final layer of sticks and pour over any remaining syrup. Leave the cake in the fridge to firm up for several hours. It softens in the fridge, which makes it easier to cut.

Scatter the sprinkles on top of the cake and decorate with the sweets. Lift the cake from the tin, using the paper.

79

Date and Honey Cake
Saudi Arabia

Generally considered to be the 'king of dates', the Medjool date is soft, plump and succulent – perfect for this cake. I happened to have a beehive tin I wanted to try out, hence the shape of the cake in the picture, but you can bake it in a square or round tin instead.
The cake has a honey and cinnamon syrup poured over it and is then returned to the oven. The first time I made it, I could hardly wait for it to cool so I could try it.

3 medium eggs
100g caster sugar
75g unsalted butter, melted
½ teaspoon vanilla extract
75g fresh Medjool dates, pitted and
  chopped
75g plain flour

Honey and cinnamon syrup
65g unsalted butter
50g caster sugar
65g honey
½ teaspoon ground cinnamon

Heat the oven to 170°C/Gas Mark 3. Grease and flour a 15cm beehive cake tin, or a shallow 20cm square tin or 18cm round tin.

Using an electric mixer, beat the eggs and sugar together for about 5 minutes, until pale, fluffy and tripled in volume. Fold in the melted butter and vanilla with a large metal spoon. Coat the dates in a little of the flour to prevent them sinking. Sift the rest of the flour and gently fold it in, followed by the dates.

Pour the mixture into the prepared cake tin and bake for 20 minutes, until the cake is golden and well risen and a skewer inserted in the centre comes out clean. Leave to cool in the tin for 10 minutes, then turn out on to a wire rack. If you have used a square or round tin, there's no need to take the cake out. Raise the oven temperature to 190°C/Gas Mark 5.

While the cake is cooling, prepare the syrup. Melt the butter in a small pan, add the rest of the ingredients and bring to the boil, stirring constantly. Pour the syrup gently over the cake, return it to the tin if using the beehive one, and put it back in the oven for 15 minutes. Let it cool completely in the tin before turning out. It is very good served warm with date ice cream.

80 Nuremberg Gingerbread House
Germany

In the eighteenth century, the popularity of the Grimm brothers' fairytale, 'Hansel and Gretel', encouraged bakers in Germany to create the first gingerbread houses, which are now associated with Christmas time.

You will find them particularly in Nuremberg, which is the gingerbread capital of the world. Traditional Nuremberg gingerbread is sweetened with honey and includes ground ginger, cinnamon, cloves, nutmeg and cardamom. My recipe is a little less complicated and I have used golden syrup to sweeten it, but if you like honey you can use that instead.

250g unsalted butter
200g dark muscovado sugar
120g golden syrup
600g plain flour
2 teaspoons bicarbonate of soda
4 teaspoons ground ginger
1 teaspoon ground mixed spice

To decorate
2 tubes of royal icing
2 boxes of Matchmakers or mini
　chocolate fingers
250g whole unblanched almonds
a few sweets, such as dolly mixtures
1 tub of edible silver glitter
1 can of silver shimmer spray
　(optional)

Heat the oven to 180°C/Gas Mark 4. Melt the butter, sugar and syrup together in a pan. Sift the flour, bicarbonate of soda and spices into a large mixing bowl. Add the warm melted butter mixture and bring together by hand to make a stiff dough. Add a little water if it won't quite come together.

It's easiest to roll the dough out on a sheet of baking parchment, as this makes it easier to transfer to baking trays. Roll out a third of the dough at a time to 11mm thick. Cut out the shapes using the templates on page 187. Slide the gingerbread shapes, still on the baking parchment, on to baking trays. You can re-roll the trimmings. If you have any spare, you can make trees, roof tiles, stars etc. for decorating the house.

Bake the pieces for 12 minutes or until golden brown and firm. If they lose their shape during baking, trim them whilst they are still warm, using a sharp knife and the template. Cool completely before assembly.

Assemble the house on a 25cm square cake card. Use the royal icing to stick the panels together, piping it along the seams and pressing them gently together until they stick. Use small cups or glasses to support the walls from the inside, then leave to dry for 3 hours before decorating.

Attach the Matchmakers or chocolate finger biscuits to the sides of the house with a little icing. Stick the almonds on to the roof with more icing. Use the sweets to decorate as you wish and then finish with piped icing on the top and sides of the roof to resemble snow. Dust the icing with the silver glitter before it dries. Spray with silver shimmer spray for a really glittering finish.

TEMPERING & PIPING

tempering chocolate

Tempering is necessary to bring chocolate back to the correct crystalline form once it has been melted. It is essential whenever you are using chocolate to make decorations or for finishing purposes, such as coating cookies and petits fours or dipping chocolate truffles. When the crystals in the chocolate are stable, it will be firm and easy to work with, whereas if it contains too many unstable crystals it will be uneven and streaky. Tempering encourages the formation of the right kind of crystals.

Successfully tempered chocolate has the following desirable properties:

• A high gloss
• A resistance to warmth
• A pleasant aroma
• A smooth mouth-feel
• A longer shelf life
• A good snap – the chocolate is crisp and snaps when broken

Undesirable qualities are:

• A white/grey colour or white streaks
• Vulnerability to warmth
• A dull appearance
• A soft, flexible consistency

Before the chocolate can be tempered, it needs to be melted. Never let it come into direct contact with the heat source: it will burn. The best way to melt it at home is in a bowl placed over a pan of gently simmering water. Here are the correct melting temperatures for chocolate:

Dark chocolate
• Melt until it reaches 40–45°C
• Cool to 27–28°C
• Reheat to a working temperature of 31–32°C

Milk chocolate
• Melt until it reaches 32.5°C
• Cool to 27–28°C

• Reheat to a working temperature of no more than 30°C

White chocolate
• Melt until it reaches 30.5°C
• Cool to 27°C
• Reheat to a working temperature of 28°C

You will need a chocolate thermometer in order to get accurate readings of the temperatures. Domestic chocolate tempering machines are available. They are not cheap but they do work very well, and are worth considering if you plan to do large amounts of chocolate work regularly at home.

Decorations made from tempered chocolate will keep for 3 months in a sealed container in the fridge. Any leftover tempered chocolate can be poured on to a piece of baking parchment, left to harden and then chopped up ready for cooking in recipes.

What follows is a step-by-step guide to tempering chocolate at home.

1. Working in a cool, draught-free environment (ideally the room temperature should be no more than 21°C), chop the chocolate as finely as you can with a large, sharp knife. Place a little over two-thirds of the chocolate into a clean bowl, preferably a metal one.

2. Place the bowl over a pan of simmering water, making sure the water does not touch the base of the bowl. There should be no water or steam coming up around the sides of the bowl (if any steam or drops of water came into contact with the chocolate, it would 'seize' and be unworkable). The water should be simmering gently, not boiling.

3. Melt the chocolate to the temperature specified above, using a chocolate thermometer to check it. Stir very gently with a spatula as it melts and do not leave it unattended at any time. When the chocolate is nearly two-thirds melted, remove the bowl from the pan of water and place it on a folded dry kitchen cloth. This prevents the bowl sitting directly on the work surface, which would cool it too quickly, and also keeps the bottom of the bowl dry.

4. Continue to stir gently; the heat of the chocolate and of the bowl will help to melt the remaining pieces of chocolate. Add a tablespoon of the remaining chopped chocolate and stir until it has melted. This process is known as seeding. Keep adding a tablespoon of the finely chopped chocolate and stirring gently.

The temperature of the chocolate will be reduced.

Be careful not to add so much chocolate that it no longer melts. The aim is to reduce the temperature of the melted chocolate by adding small, room-temperature, crystalline pieces of chocolate.

5. When the pieces of chocolate no longer melt, stop adding them. The precrystallising state has now started, the chocolate is beginning to come down in temperature and the crystals are starting to form a stable structure. The chocolate now needs to cool to a temperature of 27–28°C. If you leave the chocolate in a cool place and stir it from time to time, it will come down in temperature by itself. The amount of time it takes to do this depends on the working environment. The cooler the environment, the quicker the desirable temperature will be reached – as a rough guideline, it should take about 10–15 minutes on a normal British day or in an airconditioned room. Use the thermometer to keep a check on the temperature.

6. Once the chocolate has reached the correct temperature, it is at a stable level and fully tempered, but it is not at the best temperature for working with. So place the bowl back over the pan of simmering water and bring it up to the working temperature given above. As this is only a few degrees higher and you will be tempering a relatively small amount of chocolate, extreme caution should be taken to avoid bringing the chocolate past the ideal temperature. (If this does happen, simply restart the cooling process and bring it back down to 27–28°C.) I suggest you place the bowl back over the simmering water for only a few seconds, as it will heat up very quickly and retain enough heat to bring the chocolate past the ideal temperature. Remove the bowl after 5 seconds and stir gently, then test with the chocolate thermometer. If it is not at the correct temperature, keep placing the bowl back over the pan

of simmering water for only a few seconds at a time until the ideal temperature is reached.

7. You can test the chocolate to see if it has all the desirable qualities by dipping the tip of a knife into it and placing the knife in a cool place. It should set in an even manner, be free of white streaks and have a high shine and gloss. If it's not right, simply start the tempering process again.

8. Keep the bowl of tempered chocolate resting on the folded kitchen cloth while you work with it according to the instructions in your recipe. If it begins to cool down, you can warm it again so long as it does not go past the working temperature.

tempering chocolate in a microwave

The microwave is a fast way of tempering a small amount of chocolate (but never less than 250g) but you need to be very careful, as the chocolate is more likely to burn. Follow the steps described above but use the microwave to melt the chocolate and bring it back to working temperature. It is vital that the microwave is on half power. Melt the chocolate gradually, just a few minutes at a time and, when you are trying to achieve the working temperature, just a few seconds at a time. Stir the chocolate frequently during the melting process.

using a piping bag

1. Until you become skilled in using a piping bag, it does help to cut off the end of the bag to insert the piping nozzle. Cut the bag, insert the nozzle, then fold the bag back where the nozzle is and secure with a bulldog clip to keep it in place, so nothing can leak out.

2. Fold back the top of the piping bag over your left hand (assuming you are right handed) and make the opening as wide as possible. For beginners, this can be

done by placing the bag in a large measuring jug and folding the top of the bag over the rim of the jug; this leaves both hands free to fill the bag.

3. Fill the bag using a spoon or ladle, but take care not to fill it too high; about half way is sufficient. If the bag is too full, it will be difficult to control.

4. Take the bag from the jug and seal the top by bringing the opening together and twisting it closed. Clench it tightly in your right hand, making sure your hand is sitting firmly around the top of the bag where it meets the filling. This is very important, as the pressure needs to come from the top of the bag. If you squeeze from the middle, the mix above your hand will travel up the bag and come out of the top, which is not being held closed by your hand.

5. Now hold the bag pointing downwards towards the baking sheet or vessel you are filling and squeeze gently. This needs to be a controlled motion. The more firmly you squeeze, the quicker the mix will come out of the bag. Do not squeeze the bag until it is in the glass or 2.5cm from the baking sheet. To stop the mix coming out, simply stop the pressure and lift the tip of the bag upwards.

6. As the bag empties, remember to move your grip on the top of the bag so it is always firmly on top of the mix.

A good way to practise is to use Trex or other vegetable shortening. It is soft enough to pipe straight from the fridge but firm enough to control. Simply pipe out different shapes, such as buns or fingers, on a worktop. You can keep scraping it up and refilling the bag for as long as it takes to master the art.

making a paper piping bag

If you are piping small amounts of chocolate, you can make a paper piping bag, as follows:

1. Cut out a rectangle of baking parchment approximately 25 x 20cms. Cut the rectangle in half diagonally to make 2 triangles.

2. Using one triangle, place it flat on the work surface so the right angle of the triangle is pointing towards your right elbow (assuming you are right handed). Curl the top point over to meet the right angle and form a cone shape.

3. Wrap the remaining long side around the outside of the cone, making sure the point of the cone doesn't come open.

4. Fold the points over twice to secure the cone.

Remember not to overfill the piping bag with chocolate, or it will be difficult to handle and will come out of the top of the bag. After filling the bag, roll the top down to secure the chocolate inside whilst piping. Snip the pointed end of the cone to make a small opening – the wider the opening, the thicker the chocolate piping will be.

TEMPLATES

This is the template for the components of the Gingerbread House on page 180. Cut out two of each of the shapes shown here, to size, to create the pieces for your house.

roof panels

front and back walls

side walls

SUPPLIERS

Most of the ingredients and equipment used in this book are readily available in supermarkets and high-street shops. Below are some recommended online stockists for more specialist items.

Almond Art

www.almondart.com
Phone 01255 223322

Soft confectioner's fondant, sprinkles, edible glitters and lustre sprays, gold and silver leaf, cake cards, acetate transfer sheets

The Asian Cookshop

www.theasiancookshop.co.uk

Pandan essence, also known as kewra water

Bakery Bits

www.bakerybits.co.uk
Phone 01404 565656

Pandoro tins, wooden baking moulds, plus a large range of loaf tins and cake tins, including angel food cake and bundt tins

Dr Oetker

www.oetkeronline.co.uk
Phone 0113 823 1401

Sprinkles, gel food colourings, wafer butterflies, shimmer sprays, coloured icing

Healthy Supplies

www.healthysupplies.co.uk
Phone 0800 0272 616

Natural food colourings, including beetroot powder, plus coconut flakes, freeze-dried raspberries and other fruits

House of Sugar

www.houseofsugar.co.uk
Phone 01981 259999

Sugarpaste decorations, including bees, ladybirds and flowers

Kitchens

www.kitchenscookshop.co.uk
Phone 029 2022 7899

A wide selection of caking baking and decorating equipment, including a good selection of bundt tins

Lakeland

www.lakeland.co.uk
Phone 015394 88100

Individual card cake cases and loaf cakes, bundt tins, topsy-turvy cake tins, dome (hemisphere) cake tins, a variety of silicone moulds including cake pop moulds, flowerpot moulds, and chocolate teacake moulds. Also Candy Melts, strawberry flavouring and a range of food colourings and cake decorations

Sprinkles Shop

www.sprinklesshop.co.uk
Phone 01475 674840

Specialises in sprinkles, sugar flowers and dragees

INDEX

ACKNOWLEDGEMENTS

Thanks to everyone at Absolute Press: to Jon Croft and Meg Avent for another wonderful opportunity (I hope there are more to come!); to Matt Inwood for the wonderful design and for going above and beyond keeping me calm and collected; and to Alice for keeping me to deadlines and for baking the recipes before they were even edited and thinking they were great.

At Bloomsbury, thank you to Ellen Williams and Anna Bowen for their sterling work bringing this book to the attention of so many.

Special thanks to Jane Middleton, who had the mammoth task of editing my recipes and did so gracefully with bucket-loads of patience.

Thank you to Jean Cazals for the stunningly beautiful and amazing photography, and to Jo Harris for providing all the props to show off the cakes at their best.

Bountiful thanks to Mike Lucy, who has supported me throughout the making of this book and allowed me access to a kitchen and ingredients. And to Sanjay Gour and his team: Andree, Richard, Sahara, Fabio, Rotua, Alasdair Beach, Nathan Jones and Almaz for putting up with me in their space. Special thanks to Fabio for his help in purchasing a pandoro mould all the way from Italy; Rotua for helping me make the base for the Kiev cake; and Nathan Jones for whipping up a base when I didn't have time. Thanks to Louise Rigden for her support and love. And not forgetting Jennie Brotherston, who came to my rescue by kindly lending me her kransekake rings!

Thanks to my team of home bakers, who have tirelessly tested the recipes: Karen Glasse, my next-door neighbour, who baked the most and must be truly glad her baking marathon is over; the lovely David Cox, who made valuable notes and fed his family copious amounts of cake; and, of course, Holly.

My friends who have given me recipes from their mothers, families and friends from one end of the world to the other, thank you all!

Special thanks to two suppliers who posted items to me express for photography needs at the last minute without hesitation: Marilyn at MPP Designs for the wafer butterflies and Fiona at Sprinkles Shop for the icing flowers, bless you both.

Lastly and by no means least, unending thanks to André Bieganski and my family – Mum, Dad, Vince and Kirsten – for being there and understanding when I was tired, miserable, unresponsive and unavailable to be the daughter, sister and companion they needed me to be.